THE
FIG LEAF
CHRONICLES

HIDING FROM GOD
IN THE MODERN WORLD

THE
FIG LEAF
CHRONICLES

HIDING FROM GOD
IN THE MODERN WORLD

DEB GORMAN

Edited by Dori Harrell, Breakout Editing
Cover design by Emilie Haney
Author's photograph by Ric Brunstetter, RBIII Studios
Formatting by Colleen Jones

ISBN 979-8-9906691-0-9 (Paperback)
ISBN 979-8-9906691-1-6 (Digital)

Published by Deb Gorman
Debo Publishing
https://debggorman.com

Contents

For our first parents . . .
Sometimes lessons come the hard way.

ACKNOWLEDGMENTS

So many people to thank . . . where to begin is the question. First and foremost is Yahweh, my Father. He was present in the garden with our first parents when they became living beings under His creative hands. He watched them get to know each other, to work together, to fall in love with each other.

And then one day He watched as their eyes were opened to something He never planned for them to see—evil. And His eyes drifted to the tree of life and He knew what had to be done. Someday He would have to take their place (and mine) on another tree. He started planning the creation of that tree right then and there, I think.

Moving on to the here and now, I thank my family and my friends, who know me and still put up with me.

I thank my editor, Dori Harrell, for her excellent and talented administrations to my rough words and for her constant encouragement.

I thank the many people who ask me, "Deb, what are you writing now?" Sometimes that question throws me, because there are the projects actually on my hard drive . . . but there are so many that haven't yet made it to the screen. They're still in my head looking for a way out.

And that's scary.

I read this quote once, attributed to Stephen King, the king of scary: "The scariest moment is always just before you start."

I'll be sure to let you know the next time I get scared.

And they were both naked, the man and his wife, and were not ashamed.
Genesis 2:25

And they sewed fig leaves together and made themselves coverings.
Genesis 3:7

*So they sewed fig leaves together
and made coverings for themselves.*
Genesis 3:7

INTRODUCTION

T his is a book about hiding from God.

You'd think we would have learned by now that we can't, but we're a stubborn species. And we learned from the best.

Our first parents gave us the template when they disobeyed God in the only *thou shalt not command* He gave them.

You heard right—only one. He gave them many *thou shalt* commands, but only one negative.

Adam and Eve had one job—stay away from *that* tree. Eat anything else you want, but not from *that* tree. You'd think . . . Well, we can armchair quarterback all we want, but the truth is this:

> In their place, in that time, with that temptation,
> we would do the same.
> No discussion.

Afterward, when they heard God moving softly through the garden calling their names, they threw their plan together on the fly.

You see, they'd looked at each other and realized they stood naked—they'd thrown away the God-made coverings of righteousness He'd given them in favor of the flimsy offering of a thrill ride into the dark abyss of disobedience.

What to do . . . what to do.

They had to cover up and do it quickly.

They grabbed what was closest and wrapped the leaves around themselves, foolishly thinking God wouldn't notice. The same God who'd made them *and* the leaves. Really?

Fast-forward to the twenty-first century.

Our leaves may look a bit different, but they're still just leaves—no match for the robes of righteousness God intended us to wear. And those fig leaves we reach for have become more and more of a necessity. After all, we can't be expected to actually look God in the eye and admit what we've done, right?

When the first couple sinned, it was a big deal—on the order of a nuclear bomb dropped on the paradise God had created for them. Not so with us.

Since we live with, breathe, and digest sin each and every day in this modern world, it has become no big deal.

Back to the fig leaves.

I have a mental closet full of the tattered things, and I still find myself reaching for them when I can't bring myself to admit to God that I'm hiding from Him—again.

Let's talk about the ways we hide from God in the modern world.

And for goodness' sake, let's give Adam and Eve a break—stop blaming them every time we don our leaves. My decision to disobey is not their fault. It's mine.

It's time to swing wide the closet door and do some spring cleaning.

Now Martha said to Jesus, "Lord, if You had been here, my brother would not have died."
John 11:21

The Fig Leaf of
HIDING BEHIND SORROW

God, if you had been there, my sister would not have died. Can you believe I said that to the ever-present, every-where-present Creator of the cosmos?

I did. I sounded just like Mary and Martha in John 11. Lazarus, their beloved brother, had fallen ill, and they'd sent for Jesus. Jesus loved Lazarus, and the two sisters expected Him to drop everything and come running to his bedside.

But He didn't. He didn't arrive until four days *after* Lazarus's death. Jesus missed the funeral, the burial in the family tomb, the grief-laden tears of Mary and Martha. He missed it all. And those two sisters let Him know how they felt about that.

When my sister died by her own hand in 1989, I assumed God had missed it all.

The drive to Montana from her home in the Seattle area, with the gun hidden in her vehicle. Checking in at the motel. The last moments of her life.

I couldn't put together why God didn't know where she went and what she planned to do. Did He not have a map of the United States? Hadn't He created the world and the place she chose? Couldn't the God who thought her up have stopped her from ending herself?

Where was He when she decided life wasn't worth it?

Where was He when I wallowed in guilt for not paying attention? For not knowing my sister was helpless to help herself?

Where was He when I had to tell my three young children their favorite aunt was gone and answer their agonizing questions? I still see their wide-eyed faces and tears slipping down their cheeks.

Where was He when my older brother and I looked at each other and realized we'd lost another sibling, our younger brother having been killed in a traffic accident five years prior?

Where was He when our parents, having outlived two children within five years, collapsed under the weight of heartbreaking sorrow and pain, then finally going their separate ways after more than forty years of being inseparable?

Our close-knit family ties were shredded. A family of six was now four in the space of such a short time. We each now paddled our own canoes, unable to help ourselves, let alone each other.

I spent the next several years hiding from God behind my self-made personal fig leaf. How did I do that?

I had a whole wardrobe of fig leaves, labeled on the stems.

- *Stop going to church*, where the only question had become, "Deb, how are you doing?" How do you answer that without collapsing in a puddle of grief or wrapping your hands around the throat of the other person, because it's the fifteenth time you've heard the question that day?

- *Stop talking* to the One who could've done something—the One who thought me up.

- *Distance myself* from my remaining family, because we all felt guilty for not knowing, not being aware of whatever it was she was going through.

- *Refuse to be comforted or forgiven* by God or anyone else. Because accepting comfort means it's real and that my guilt is assuaged. I must cling to my guilt because that's the only way I can maintain control of my raging emotions.

And the list goes on. Each time I experienced a new emotion or memory, I made another fig leaf, labeled it, and hung it in my Fig Leaf Closet.

The problem, though, with clothing ourselves—trying to shield ourselves from the harshness of this life while blaming God—is that those fig leaves are entirely inadequate. Our first parents certainly discovered this.

When God talked them out of their hiding place, wearing their meager vegetation, they couldn't even look at Him in their embarrassment.

Only *His* clothing—woven by His own sacrifice—will cover us with His protection, His wisdom, His understanding of human existence. Only by laying down the hardness—the grief, the frantic attempts to put a name to what He has allowed—and letting Him gently guide us through the cracks in our hearts will we at last come to the place, that sweet place, of total trust in Him.

He asks us to trust Him with ourselves and our loved ones.

It's not a onetime proposition.

Each time we're swamped by life on this planet, we must choose again to shed our homemade fig leaves, come out from behind our self-erected walls, and run into His arms.

If we do this, we'll be amazed at how easily those fig leaves can be discarded.

And by how wholly inadequate they were.

Questions for Personal Reflection

1. What personal sorrow are you hiding behind? Finish this sentence: *God, if You'd been there,*

   _____

   _____

   _____

   _____

2. Look at the labels on my fig leaves. What are the labels on the stems of your Hiding Behind Sorrow fig leaves?

   _____

   _____

   _____

   _____

3. The Bible teaches that God is sovereign, all powerful, and all knowing. God knew about and allowed this sorrow to invade this space called Your Life. How does understanding this truth change your perspective regarding your sorrow? And what will you do about it?

   _____

   _____

   _____

   _____

But it displeased Jonah exceedingly,
and he became angry.
Jonah 4:1

The Fig Leaf of
HIDING BEHIND EXCUSES

H as God ever asked you, *What are you doing here?* Yes?
Me too.

The question has not always sounded the same—depending on which word God emphasizes.

For instance, *What are **you** doing here*? Or, *What are you doing **here***? See the difference? I've heard both versions.

When we don our fig leaves, trying to cover up, there's no telling where we might end up.

Consider Jonah.

He was minding his own business one day, in his hometown near Jerusalem, and received an astonishing and disturbing message from God.

Arise, go to Nineveh, that great city, and cry out against it;
for their wickedness has come up before Me.

Jonah did what any red-blooded Hebrew would do. He ran
for his life. Why?

Think of it.

God told him to go preach to a godless nation, one that had a
reputation for brutality, especially against God's people. They were
infamous in their day for torturing their enemies, the enslavement
of women and children, and other conscienceless atrocities.

Jonah had grown up with the stories, had probably witnessed
some of them.

Nineveh was northeast of Jerusalem. Jonah packed up and
went west—to a seaport named Joppa—and boarded a ship bound
for Tarshish. The precise location of Tarshish isn't known, but it
was in the opposite direction of Jonah's God-given assignment.

He ran because he was afraid of those barbarians. Anyone
would be afraid, right? But there was a deeper issue in play.

Jonah knew the power of God—and if God told him to go
preach to the Assyrians, there was a good chance some might
believe and escape judgment.

Thinking of that possibility sealed his rebellious plan. No
way would he be party to those cruel folks being given a chance
to repent. Jonah was a very human guy.

He knew the power of God, but did he know the full extent
of it? I think not . . . else Jonah would not have run in the opposite direction, thinking to escape God's plan, and then end up in
the belly of a monstrous sea creature. He also discovered God's
power and His sense of humor at the same time.

Sense of humor? Yes.

Jonah refused to kneel himself and take on God's assignment with joy. Instead, God placed him in the innards of a fish,
where it was kneeling room only.

From that God-made prayer room, Jonah finally gave up his fight and agreed to go on mission to Assyria.

And speaking of God's sense of humor, there was no heroic escape from the fish for Jonah. No, God made the fish sick to its stomach, and it vomited Jonah out—yuck!—and Jonah wretched up on shore, no doubt reeking of that creature's last dinner.

After that stinky experience, Jonah agreed to get back on the path God had for him and stop lurking in the shadows of faith. He pointed his steps northwest again.

How many times do I lurk in the shadows of my faith, afraid to be seen?

Not take a stand for fear of offending? For fear of appearing quack-like? Afraid of being labeled a conspiracy theorist, a racist, a hater?

The Fig Leaves of Excuses I wrap around myself cannot hide my cowardice or my shame. And consider this: at least for now, I don't have to fear what Jonah feared. Most of my angst is self-made, wanting to fit in, not stand out.

See? There's Jesus now, standing just across my hometown courtyard of public opinion, beckoning me to come into the light. Not to make *myself* known though.

No, to make *Him* known—the one who refused to back down, give up, or give in to the religious leaders of his day.

Why would He do that?

To make sure that I, Deb Gorman, would hear about Him in 1968 and choose to follow. And to make sure that you would have the opportunity to hear the gospel.

That we would be gifted the choice to trade our Excuse-Laden Fig Leaves for His clothes steeped in righteousness and that our voices would thunder with conviction, leading our generation, or the neighbor down the street, or our family member, to faith in God.

Let's not go to Tarshish, okay? Let's head down the path He chooses for us. There might be whales lurking out there, waiting to be used of God to send us back in His direction.

Questions for Personal Reflection

1. When was the last time you ran away from God, and why did you run? Where did you end up?

    _____

    _____

    _____

    _____

2. Did you keep running, or did you—like Jonah—kneel inside your giant fish and give up your struggle?

    _____

    _____

    _____

    _____

3. Or are you still running? Do you think it's time to stop?

    _____

    _____

    _____

    _____

He said to him,
"Do you want to be made well?"
John 5:6

The Fig Leaf of
HIDING FROM HEALING

Have you ever asked a question of your teenager and gotten a roundabout answer that didn't really qualify as an answer?

"Where have you been? It's one in the morning."

"Out."

"Where?"

"I just drove over to Pete's house, that's all."

"I called Pete's parents. You weren't there. And Pete was already asleep."

"Well . . ."

And so it goes.

In John 5:6–7 Jesus asks a simple question of a man who'd been infirm for a long while: "Do you want to be made well?"

Of course, Jesus didn't ask because He didn't know the answer. He asked to make sure the man knew who *had* the answer. God never asks questions to *gain* information—He asks in order to reveal truth. In this instance, it was essential the man be confronted with his need.

Has God ever asked you a question? I know—mostly it's us asking the questions, right? Perhaps it would behoove us to listen closely in the cracks of our prayer lives—in order to hear God asking us questions. Then maybe, in answering His question, we might discover a truth He wants us to understand or a direction we should go.

The curious thing about this story of Jesus and the man with a longtime infirmity is that the man didn't answer the question. He dodged it. He could've just said *Yes—heal me!* Instead He gave Jesus a bunch of details about his daily struggles, details Jesus already knew. Why did he do that?

I've never done that . . . have you?

Okay, yes I have.

Deb, why did you say such a hurtful thing to her?
God, did you hear what she said to me?

Deb, why don't you trust Me with that? It's too heavy for you.
God, why did you allow that to happen to me?

Deb, come and sit in my lap . . . let me heal you from that.
God, what will happen after that?

Why do we hide from healing? Why do we skirt the issues that bring disease into our lives?

Let's face it—healing is hard work. It's scary. When we hand over the *heal me* reins to God, we give up control. Could that be the real issue—we have to give up control?

I have an idea.

Let's commit to *just answer the question* when Jesus asks us what we want Him to do for us. Let's stop with the evasiveness and misdirection. Let's stop saying to the Lord of the universe, *I don't want to go that way with You—let's go this way instead. Less rocks, less drop-offs, less chance I'll get hurt, less chance I'll have to drop my leaves.*

Whether it's a modern-life problem (finances, illness, broken relationship) or a sin we just can't deal with on our own (one of those why-did-I-do-that-again? sins that bedevil us), let's open our empty hands and let God fill them with His healing and goodness.

Let's just answer His question, shall we? Then be sure to listen to His answer.

Questions for Personal Reflection

1. Has God asked you any questions lately? If so, why do you think He's asking those questions? (Remember, He already knows the answers.) List the questions below.

   _____
   _____
   _____
   _____

2. Now, list your answers. If you haven't answered Him, perhaps now is a good time.

   _____
   _____
   _____
   _____

3. What did God reveal to you as you answered His questions?

   _____
   _____
   _____
   _____

As for God, His way is perfect.
2 Samuel 22:31

The Fig Leaf of
HIDING BEHIND PERFECTION

I came to Christ when I was fourteen and began singing solos and in groups at fifteen. I came by my talent naturally on my mother's side. In college I received formal vocal training and went on to be a soloist at Christian-led events and in churches for the next four decades. I believed God had given me a music ministry, and I loved, in a scared sort of way, being in front of an audience.

That was then. This is now.

In 2008 I developed a serious double ear infection that robbed me of about 30 percent of my hearing. A vocalist who cannot hear cannot sing in groups, because she must be able to hear the other singers if a good blend is to be achieved.

I stopped singing altogether. At first I missed it. But now, not so much. *Why?* you ask.

Looking back over my years as a vocalist, I now admit that what I was doing was not worship of the One. It was Deb worship. How do I know?

Because if I messed up, if I sang a wrong word or note, I would drown in embarrassment, unable to look anyone in the eye. Does that sound like worship music to you?

The humorous part is that 99 percent of folks in an audience listening to a performance don't even know when one of those minuscule mistakes are made.

The bottom line is that yes, God had called me to use my gift of voice to lead others in worship of Him, but what it became was what God calls *blasphemous* and *contemptible*, just like Aaron's two sons offering profane fire before the Lord in Leviticus 10:1. It became about me instead of Him.

May it never again be about me but ever about His perfections.

Perfectionism allowed to run rampant has a curious outcome in the perfectionist's life. Instead of perfecting us, it sometimes kills us. Many suicides happen because the perpetrator/victim cannot live with a mistake he or she made.

Instead of allowing Christ's perfections to shine through us, we choose to depend upon our own, which plays us right into the Enemy's hands.

Let's take a break here and examine our Fig Leaf Closets. Let's jerk out the one labeled Hiding Behind Perfection, rip it to shreds, and put it where it belongs.

Into the hands of Jesus the Christ, the only perfect One.

Questions for Personal Reflection

1. In what ways are you a perfectionist? How does perfectionism affect your relationships?

   _____

   _____

   _____

   _____

2. What ways has your perfectionism made you self-reliant instead of God-reliant? Write a list.

   _____

   _____

   _____

   _____

3. What must you do in your life to eradicate perfectionism from it, in order to rely only upon the strengths of your perfect Savior? Will you commit to doing what it takes?

   _____

   _____

   _____

   _____

And His disciples asked Him, saying,
"Rabbi, who sinned, this man or his parents,
that he was born blind?"
John 9:1, 2

The Fig Leaf of
HIDING BEHIND MYSELF

W hy was I born this way?

This question was subtly asked in the John 9. Some disciples asked Jesus why a certain man was born blind. Good question, to be sure, but they went on to assume it was because of the sin of the man or his parents.

Jesus set them straight about that.

The man was born blind in order to showcase God's power.

And the same is true of us.

I know . . . I know. Some say, "How can God be good if He allows _____ to be part of my life?"

Here's a verse to consider: "For as the heavens are higher than the earth, so are My ways higher than your ways, and My thoughts than your thoughts" (Isaiah 55:9).

When I look at my lack of height—I've always wanted to be three or four inches taller—I ask myself why couldn't I have been born taller. Or better looking. Or blond. Or with perfect sight. And the list goes on.

Some folks ask the question differently.

How can God be good if He allowed cancer to strike? Or financial ruin? Or a child, lovingly reared, to run afoul of the law and end up in prison? Or lies to be told about me?

Or ...

It's easy to wear the fig leaf of How Can God Be Good If ... It's quick to put on, quick to bring up in conversation, and it is usually received with sympathy and pats on the back.

How can God be good if ...

How would you finish that sentence?

Let's get back to the way Jesus answered His disciples when they asked if the man had been born blind because of his or his parents' sin.

He was born blind in order to showcase the power and mercy of God.

How was God's power and mercy revealed in this man? Jesus healed him—and the man told people who'd healed him.

Sometimes when we're hit with life's harshness, we wave our fig leaves and say something like, "If this is the way God's gonna treat me, just forget it. I don't have to take this."

But hang on a minute. What does that get us?

Nothing. We slam the door in the face of the One who knows the end from the beginning of our lives, and as we tighten our belts around our fig leaves to keep them from slipping and revealing our utter nakedness, we are left without the loving mercy of the Lord. We are left completely to ourselves, alone and helpless to deal with what God has already offered to handle for us.

Best to say with Jesus, as we peel off those ragged leaves and discard them where the sun doesn't shine, *this* _____ *is to show off God and His mercy to a dying world.*

We'll never be sorry if we do.

Questions for Personal Reflection

1. Speaking of your*self*, would you rather have a different one?

   _____

   _____

   _____

   _____

2. What would that different you look like? How would that different you act?

   _____

   _____

   _____

   _____

3. Would that different you showcase God's strength in your weakness? Or would it showcase you instead?

   _____

   _____

   _____

   _____

He has shown you, O man, what is good. And what
does the LORD *require of you But to do justly,*
To love mercy, And to walk humbly with your God.
Micah 6:8

The Fig Leaf of
HIDING BEHIND RELIGION

But religion is good, right? Churches teach religion; schools teach religion. And what about all that religion in the Bible?

Let's get to the nuts and bolts, though, of the tattered Fig Leaf of Religion versus the pure, clean robes of the gospel.

- *Religion* says: Do this and this and this. Don't do that and that and that. Wash, rinse, repeat—and you will be saved. Unless you screw up. If you screw up, start over. *The gospel* says: Christ is all I need. He has already done everything necessary to save me. All I have to do is say yes to Him and take His hand.

- *Religion* says: You need a barrier to hide behind, and that can be religion. But it's not a concrete wall. It's an easily shredded fig leaf. Just try to tell another person how wonderful your religion is and most likely you'll be shot down and walked away from. Why? Because religion doesn't care about the other person. *The gospel* says: The gospel message is not a hiding place. It should be announced—loudly—to the world. The gospel is a launchpad for God's love. The tenets of the gospel reek of love, mercy, and grace, spilling over and filling the heart of the broken seeker. Why? Because central to the gospel is God on the cross—dying an unimaginable death so we can enjoy an unimaginable heaven, safe from religion for all of eternity.

- *Religion* is a stone. A rock to stumble over. A stone to crush us. A wall to divide us. Religion is a hierarchy of flawed human beings dying in one-upmanship, forged in ego run rampant and built upon a foundation of rules to follow. Religion spawns a tyranny of death. *The gospel* is a tree of life. This life is offered to anyone who asks. The gospel, instead of crushing and breaking us, heals and unites us. Instead of being built upon the ego and tyranny of flawed human beings, the gospel is built upon the One perfect being in the universe.

In summary, *religion* is man's idea of how to live. *The gospel* is God's idea of how to live forever.

The greatest defeat in all of human history was Adam and Eve choosing to sew fig leaves together to hide from the One who'd rather die than give up his children to hell forever. And then He did.

In that moment of agonizing death, with mobs of His killers surrounding Him on that hill, *religion* was defeated and *the gospel* was born.

We must strip off the fig leaves of *religion* and wrap ourselves up in *the gospel* clothes.

We must stop hiding behind *religion* and walk out into the light of the *gospel*, scattering its seed as we go.

Questions for Personal Reflection

1. Define religion in your life. How's it working for you?

   _____

   _____

   _____

   _____

2. When you speak to a friend or loved one about Jesus, is your speech heavy with religion or relationship? Explain.

   _____

   _____

   _____

   _____

3. How can you change your focus from the Religion of Rules to the Gospel of Love? Determine to make a plan today.

   _____

   _____

   _____

   _____

Then Jesus said, "Father, forgive them,
for they do not know what they do."
Luke 23:34

The Fig Leaf of
HIDING BEHIND HURT

The deep pain of a close family member's cutting off a relationship is not one to be experienced by the faint of heart. And not knowing why, no explanations, just a texted *don't ever contact me again* hacks deep into the heart. It made me question everything about my faith. It made me scour every memory I had of my loved one, trying to come up with a reason, something I could fix.

Hurt must be one of humanity's most common denominators, wouldn't you agree?

Emotional hurt, physical hurt, spiritual hurt—all of us could make a bullet-point list of the ways we've been hurt (and hurt others) from cradle to whatever age we are today.

And we know there's healing for hurt, don't we? When we're hurt physically—in some ways the easiest hurt to deal with—we see a doctor or take a medicine. When we experience emotional hurt, sometimes it helps to talk it out with a trusted friend or family member. Pastors and other clergy are the go-to people for spiritual hurt, although unfortunately, they are sometimes the source of spiritual hurt.

It's easy to spot physical healing, isn't it? We can breathe better, the headache goes away, and the wound scabs over.

But what does healing from emotional hurt or spiritual hurt look like?

Is there a gash on my heart that stops bleeding?

Or a broken part of my mind that starts working again?

Or how about being able to breathe the air of love again after the suffocation of emotional trauma?

I don't know about you, but this all sounds scary. Scary because it's easier to hide behind my fig leaves than to come out from behind them, exposing my naked pain for all to see. Scary because maybe it's my fault somehow that I hurt, that I caused that person to hurt me.

I'd rather grab that fig leaf labeled It Hurts, wrap it around myself, and pretend I feel nothing.

But God has a different idea about that.

He's waiting on the other side of my closet door. He implores me to discard that fig leaf called It Hurts and let Him clothe me in His pure robe called Compassion. To sit down with Him and talk it over.

And when I do what He wants, when I choose to be present with Him in my pain, He opens my eyes to more. He lets me see the other side of the coin. The possibility that maybe, just maybe, the one who hurt me hurts also.

It's been said that hurt people hurt people.

Perhaps God allows us to experience hurt in order to open a door of dialogue with Him, to have a back-and-forth, and then to intercede for the other person's hurt.

Shredding another fig leaf now. Leaving the fragments behind, then allowing God to re-dress me, I hear the creak of the closet door as it closes behind me.

Across the path I see a table set for two with the One already seated, nail-scarred hand beckoning me into the chair next to Him.

I sit and pour out my heart to Him about the one who has slammed the door.

He doesn't chide me, tell me to be nice, or blame me, nor does He even interrupt me.

He listens. He holds my hand. He leans into my face and looks into my eyes.

And when I am spent with my heartbreak, He sits back, hands folded in His lap, and proposes a new thought.

Perhaps, Deb, this isn't about you. What a concept, right?

Then He gently asks me, *What would you like Me to do for your friend or loved one?*

With that one question, He helps me see the other person as a cherished soul who needs rescue, not as the other half of a soured relationship to be discarded.

Let's not hide from God when someone hurts us.

Let's allow Him to expose it to our souls for what it is: an opportunity.

For prayer, for personal growth, to become more like Jesus.

Instead of reaching for the Fig Leaf of Hiding Behind Hurt, allowing the hurt to fester and grow into bitterness, let's practice going to Him first and learning to see others—even those who hurt us—through His eyes.

Questions for Personal Reflection

1. How have you been hurt or betrayed by someone you cherish? How long have you carried the hurt?

   _____

   _____

   _____

   _____

2. What are the symptoms and side effects you've experienced from this hurt or betrayal?

   _____

   _____

   _____

   _____

3. What have you done to heal from this hurt? (Please note: we have to heal before seeking reconciliation with the other person.)

   _____

   _____

   _____

   _____

*But Jesus said to him, "Follow Me, and
let the dead bury their own dead."*
Matthew 8:22

The Fig Leaf of
HIDING BEHIND WORK

B ut, you say, work is good.
God tells us to work with our hands, to do what we find
to do, to not be lazy, and . . .

God does say all of that in His Word, and more. I agree.
Work is good.

It keeps us focused on providing for our families, on helping others, on managing our time well in order to get stuff done.

But . . . as Jesus told the man in the verse above, following
Him should be *the* priority—not getting all our self-assigned
work done before we take that step.

I'm working as I write these words. I try to maintain a
quota of words to type on the page five days a week. My goal
is a thousand words, five days a week. Five thousand words in

the typical M–F workweek. That sounds like a lot, but it really isn't—it's only four pages per day, give or take.

I usually try to get those thousand words done prior to doing anything else at my desk. And it doesn't matter what document I spill the words on. It could be emails, responding to a blog post, editing a manuscript, or social media posting on my author platforms. As long as I'm typing words, it counts toward my thousand-word goal.

Ahem! Did you see what I just did? Two paragraphs, 135 words, about writing words.

What's wrong with that? you ask. I'll tell you what's wrong with that.

This short piece is about Hiding Behind Work. And that's what I just did. I grabbed my fig leaf labeled Work and used it to hide from God, because I'm supposed to write words that expose that nakedness.

I've worked in various job, from age fourteen to sixty-five. I've been retired from the *going*-to-work crowd since June of 2020. Now I'm part of the *staying*-home-to-work crowd. I like it a lot better. But the rules are the same. The fig leaf labeled Work can be worn in either setting.

When I worked outside the home, my most difficult task was leaving work at work. I often carried it home, which sometimes made it difficult to live in the present with my husband and children. I worried about something I'd said to a coworker—how my words might have hurt or how they were perceived. I stewed about tasks left undone and how it would add to my work load the next day.

The result? My ears didn't always hear what my children said to me about their day. I missed their fears, their hurts . . . because I was focused on me. Or I was too tired from my day to connect with my husband's day.

That's my story.

I've heard of other folks who volunteer for extra hours just to get away from home life, for whatever reason. Or those who chase the almighty dollar to the detriment of family relationships. Always under the guise of providing for them, you understand.

But spouses and children need different provision. They need our presence, our touch, our heart, our ears, and our smiles.

I can never get back the hours I wasn't present for my family. No matter how hard I might try to make up for those precious hours, do-overs are impossible.

And it's the same for everyone who has ever drawn breath on planet Earth. No matter what age we live in, what continent we inhabit, lost hours with loved ones will always remain . . . lost. We will never get a second chance with them.

Now, in my present job of writing, it's the same. I have a word-count goal to meet—but I also have a husband, brother, and a father. We have children and grandchildren who, though they may not admit it, watch us. Some of them might even take notes.

I do want to meet my word-count goal each day, but how much do I want to meet it?

So much that I'll say *no* to an outing, a visit, a dinner together? Will I really say, "Sorry, can't attend—I haven't met my goal today." Heaven forbid.

I don't want to see this on my tombstone:

Here lies Deb Gorman—
Daughter, Sister, Wife, Mom, and Grandmother.
We didn't know her, And she didn't know us.
But she always met her word-count goal.

Let's have a bonfire with this one. I'll bring my Hiding Behind Work Fig Leaf, you bring yours . . . and maybe someone can bring hot dogs.

Questions for Personal Reflection

1. Ouch! This one's hard, right? What Work leaf do you hide behind?

    _____

    _____

    _____

    _____

2. What do you envision on your tombstone—figuratively speaking—if you make no life changes? What do you want to see on your tombstone?

    _____

    _____

    _____

    _____

3. How do you see your relationships changing when you begin making those needed changes?

    _____

    _____

    _____

    _____

Oh, magnify the LORD with me, and
let us exalt His name together.
Psalm 34:3

The Fig Leaf of
HIDING BEHIND REPUTATION

A good reputation is a desirable thing, right? We don't want to go through life with a tarnished one. My parents spent a lot of time in my growing-up years talking about humility, integrity, and honesty—the bedrocks of a good reputation.

God has a lot to say, especially in Proverbs, about maintaining a good reputation. But let's dig in a bit. There might be more to a good reputation than we realize.

Remember Haman? No?

Let me refresh your memory.

Haman's story takes place around 483–473 BC in the nation of Persia. His ancestor, a thousand years before, was King Agag, who'd tried to wipe out the Jewish people and ended up tangling with Samuel, the prophet of the God of Israel. Samuel killed him. Haman, ten centuries later, held a deep-seated hatred of the Jews, many of whom had been born in Persia and were living there under Persian rule.

Haman was a guy who was super concerned about his reputation as the Persian king's go-to aide. King Ahasuerus depended on Haman and his underlings to keep his kingdom running smoothly so he could concentrate on important stuff, like whether or not his wife, Queen Vashti, would show up for the evening's entertainment.

And speaking of . . . the queen chose *not* to attend one of her husband's lavish and degrading parties, which was the catalyst leading up to the events in the book of Esther.

Who is Esther?

Esther was a secret Jew who was born in Persia. At the beginning of the story, she was pretty much a beautiful nobody who wound up replacing Vashti as queen.

But Haman found out about her lineage and used that knowledge to set about a second attempt to wipe out the Jewish race.

He put his plan in action, but things . . . well, they didn't go according to *his* plan.

At the climax of the story, Haman, ever the conniving politician trying to increase his leverage with King Ahasuerus, builds a gallows on which to hang Mordecai, Esther's uncle. Mordecai had publicly insulted Haman's bloated ego, which would just not do in Haman's world.

Haman, however, underestimated Mordecai's God. Haman's reputation didn't matter one whit to Him, and by the time God got through with Haman, he ended up hanging on his own gallows.

I left out several juicy details. You should go read it yourself. If you do, you'll realize that reputation is important . . . but *whose* reputation?

We spend time honing our reputations, making sure we're seen by others only in the best light, that our clothes and hair are just so, and that our smiles are always in place. We shove our imperfections down where the sun doesn't shine because, like Haman, it just won't do if our secret flaws hang out there for everyone to see.

When we're in church, we shake hands with people, ask "How are you?" and answer their "How are you" with "Fine, just fine," even though things aren't just fine. When we pray aloud, we choose our words carefully so as not to let our sins and sorrows leak out from the cracks in our hearts.

After all, what good would it do to let other people in? Shouldn't they be shown how good God has been to us?

They don't need to see how we've failed. They don't need to see our struggles.

We have a reputation to maintain.

But again, just *whose* reputation should we maintain?

The book of Psalms answers that question over and over.

Here's the bulletin for us: It is *God's* reputation we should concern ourselves with. And how can I uplift *His* while trying so hard to elevate *mine*?

If I allow the folks I rub elbows with to see the real me, with my faults and sins and griefs, then tell them how my God has helped me, whose reputation gets the glory?

Or maybe I'm still waiting for His answers. That's okay too, because then I can invite those people into my life to pray with me.

Then they get to be part of the answer He gives me. They get to be part of my healing.

This is the lifeblood of the church—being present with one another, no one caring about their own ego-filled reputations—but only caring about glorifying the God whose reputation must not be tarnished in the eyes of our world.

Haman missed the mark. He cared only for two things: revenge against God's people and his own reputation.

He didn't know it, but he wore a gigantic fig leaf. If he would've stripped it off and come to God to be clothed, he wouldn't have ended his life swinging by a rope of his own making.

Let's begin afresh magnifying the reputation of the only One who matters.

Questions for Personal Reflection

1. How important is your reputation to you? What makes for a good reputation in your opinion?

   _____

   _____

   _____

   _____

2. Is maintaining your reputation all about Him or all about your pride in your reputation?

   _____

   _____

   _____

   _____

3. What attitude adjustments about *your* reputation do you need to make in order to uplift *His*?

   _____

   _____

   _____

   _____

Fear not, for I am with you;
Be not dismayed, for I am your God.
Isaiah 41:10

The Fig Leaf of
HIDING BEHIND FEAR

U h-oh! I hear the wheels grinding. This is the Big Ka-huna. The lid of Pandora's box just cracked open. The target is painted. The missile just launched and is streaking at hypersonic speed from there to here . . . and the target is us.

I'm speaking a universal language now. One word that every person ever birthed on planet Earth from Adam to the baby born one second ago knows—and would like not to know.

Fear.

But . . . we can't be afraid. God is on His throne. He wins in the end. His kids will go to live with Him forever, not ever having to cry, to hurt, to die—ever again.

Right?

Right.

Here's the $64,000 question though: What about before that?

What about at my address in the here and now?

And what about where you live?

We must admit that there's a lot to be afraid of on planet Earth. But if we could zoom out to whenever this planet was birthed by God's hand, we would have to admit that fear has always been present.

Except for one time.

And that time was before the apple's juice made a sticky trail down the chins of Adam and Eve.

Before they threw caution to the winds and took that first bite, *fear* wasn't even a word in their vocabulary.

It seems amazing that they had the run of the whole place except for that one tree, and they just had to do it. The Enemy knew them well.

As he knows me. And you.

He knows that I don't particularly want to be a god. I don't long for money and fame. I don't even want to write hundreds of bestsellers.

But he does know which buttons to push to make me deep-dive into fear—that place where I forget that God is, always was, and will forever be.

What's the fear that wipes you out? That puts you down? That place where there are no answers? The one that sends you headlong to your Fig Leaf Closet to find the perfect one to hide behind while holding God at arm's length?

I'll share mine. Here it is: I can't bear the thought of losing a child.

I watched my parents go through the miserable, never-ending pain of losing two adult children within five years of each other—my younger brother and sister—and I *know* I could not live through that.

I know myself well enough to be sure of this: If that happened, it would take the miracle-to-end-all-miracles to bring me back to Him. To regenerate faith in my heart, mind, and soul. I know I'd never want to speak to Him again if He allowed that into my life.

I'd wear that Fear fig leaf for the rest of my earthly life.

Ah, but wait.

If I think back over my life, I see little chunks of fear overcome by the power of His love. Not the big Fear, you understand. The little ones.

- Fear of aloneness
- Fear of rejection
- Fear of aging
- Fear of being laughed at

These little ones still niggle from time to time, but the great thing about getting older is I have less and less bandwidth in my mind to concern myself with them.

I remember times throughout my life when God dealt with these fears—by wrapping His large hand around my small one and leading me through the turmoil in my soul, a byproduct of fear every time.

Remembering how He melted these fears away in the past goes a long way to reassuring me of His strength to do the same in my future.

But.

Not that, God. Please, not that.

So what do I do?

There was a time when it seemed I might experience the Big One.

During those few weeks, I walked around our five acres almost every day, having a conversation with God.

Did I pray? If you could call it that. It was more like hurling accusations at the sovereign Lord of the universe, daring Him to take a child from me.

How could you do this to me? What are you thinking?

Doesn't sound like much of a prayer, does it? And please note the lack of capitalization of God's pronouns. I typed those words deliberately that way—because that was how I addressed Him at the time.

But God didn't mind. How do I know?

Because as those weeks wore on, I experienced a soul shift. I realized I was no longer shouting in His face or pounding my tiny fists on His massive chest.

After exhausting myself yelling in the face of Abba Father, I quieted and began a time of pleading, crying—*supplication*, is what the Scriptures call it.

Yes, I begged . . . but with the sure knowledge that my child was right where my child belonged and had always been. In the palm of His hand, safe and secure no matter what.

And so was I. Instead of tramping around the yard, shaking my fist in His face, I now sat in His lap, His tender hands cupping my face. His gentle voice whispering to my heart, *I know, my child. Let me take your fear. I can handle it much better than you.*

By the end of that season of fear, He'd gently unwrapped the tightest fig leaf in my collection. I could not have done that myself—the Fear leaf was wound snug and superglued to my skin. I truly did not want to let it go, because I'd become comfortable in that second skin.

If I'd tried to shed it myself, I would have bled as I peeled it off. But my Father knows just where to tug, just how much pressure to apply.

And when He was finished, He wrapped the softest robe of trust around me that I'd ever felt—tailor made just for me, the mom who not so long ago was shrieking in rage in His face.

I do not make the claim that I am healed from the ravages of fear. Far from it.

Just scan the world we live in today. Fear consumes us. Here's a few:

- Fear of going out on the streets of our cities to take care of the business of daily life
- Fear of staying home and becoming isolated . . . again
- Fear of financial ruin in these turbulent economic times
- Fear of the next new virus or disease
- Fear of angry people taking out *their* fears on us and others

And the list goes on.

God shows us, as we remember and deconstruct the fear He has brought us through, that He is able to lead us through that dark tunnel again. And again. And again.

I know He will have to take my hand again sometime, somewhere—when the Enemy of my soul tries one more time to derail my love and trust in God by showing me another fig leaf I can wear.

I choose today to stay close by His side in all weathers so I won't have far to jump when I need His lap again.

Who's ready to take that leap with me?

Questions for Personal Reflection

1. Time to share. What is the name of the fear that puts you down? Here is the place to write it, to stare at it, maybe to share it with someone.

   _____

   _____

   _____

   _____

2. If God allowed that *thing* to happen to you, what do you think you would do first?

   _____

   _____

   _____

   _____

3. And then what do you think you'd do second?

   _____

   _____

   _____

   _____

I found it necessary to write to you exhorting you to
contend earnestly for the faith.
Jude 1:3

The Fig Leaf of

HIDING BEHIND COMPLACENCY

Speaking up is uncomfortable. I get that. I'm a nonconfrontational person—just ask anyone who knows me well. I don't like debates, arguments, or discord. I would rather be offered a dish of slimy worms than enter into some discussions.

I'm probably not alone in this, although I have known folks who thrive on squabbling. Those people seem to latch on to any issue that might cause a disagreement, say a word or two, then sit back and watch everyone else jump into the fray. My MO in that situation is to back away—fast.

It seems that in these current times, controversy is available on every street corner, website, workplace, and home. We could probably create an entire book—at least three hundred pages worth, single spaced, twelve-point font—of donnybrook-ish ideas and make a killing on Amazon.

But I'm not one of those who would pay good money for that volume. I don't like facing off with other people, whether family, friend, or complete stranger. And sometimes avoidance is the right thing to do. Sometimes it's better to change the subject.

Except when it's not.

There are times when speaking up is required. When wearing the Fig Leaf of Complacency won't do. Those times when it's *God's* reputation on the line.

But before speaking up, it must be bathed in prayer. If there's no time for a full bath—if the subject arises without warning—a spritz of prayer will work.

And after prayer, what then? Fireworks?

No. Remember what our teachers and parents said to us back in the day? We must put on our listening ears.

Even if we are standing firmly on the rock of scriptural truth and the other person is a confirmed scoffer of same, with his or her feet sinking in the sand, listening comes first.

I know . . . I know. It's hard. We want to jump right in and set them straight.

But here's the truth: no one cares about our opinion unless we care about theirs first.

Harsh, I know, but it's a certainty. When speaking up is required, listening to the other person is key if those nasty, uncomfortable fireworks are to be avoided.

The times that I least like confrontation is in the family setting. All my children and stepchildren are over forty. They're adults with their own families. And here's a bulletin for me— one I have to reread frequently: most of my younglings don't think like me, most don't do life like me, and some might even think I'm certifiable.

It makes for interesting times, but that's totally okay.

I've had to come to grips with the fact that it doesn't matter that they don't share my views on controversial subjects—and there are some hairy controversial subjects in the twenty-first century, wouldn't you agree? Even ten years ago I would never have thought our culture and mores would go through such upheaval as what we're witnessing in the here and now.

And everyone has an opinion about everything.

I do.

You do.

They do.

Some of these subjects raise the hackles on the backs of our necks. Some make us angry. Some make us sad. We wonder if we'll ever be able to overcome our differences in viewpoints and perspectives.

Maybe not. But here's the thing.

When you must speak up and share your perspective on _____, make sure you understand the other person's first.

Ask questions.

Play back what was said to verify that you understand.

And when it's your turn, instead of ramming your *opinion* down the other person's throat, frame it with another question: Have you considered this? Or, Have you found this to be true in your life, as I have in mine?

These questions let your friend or family member know that the battering ram is stored away in the shed and will not be used. It reveals that you are not trying to usurp their autonomy of thought. Instead, you recognize their worth and dignity, the value of their contribution to the discussion, and that you have no wish to force a change of mind on them.

But what if the other person uses the battering ram on you, even after you have taken care to approach them with respect? What if they grab you by the nape of the neck and try to force you to change your perspective to agree with theirs?

That's when you draw a line in the sand, my friend. But not a wall . . . just a line. One that can be erased. Because the door must be kept open for both of you to meet again.

What does the line sound like?

What can you say to the other person who is demanding your capitulation—that which you cannot give? How can you answer in such a way that will maintain the other's dignity, and your own?

Here's an idea:

> I hear you, and I understand where you are coming from. There are things in your life that have led you on this journey. And there are things in my life that have led me to form my perspective on _____. I can't go with you on this path you are walking, because it does not match my beliefs. But just because I can't doesn't mean I care about you less. I hope you understand and that this will not destroy our friendship.

The words *I can't go with you* releases both parties from judgment by the other person. It frees both to continue being who they are and to appreciate who the other person is.

However.

I hate to say this, but the other person may still walk away sad or angry.

You have no control over that, so get over it. I had to.

The bottom line is that complacency is negative—it's avoidance because of the fear of rattling someone else's cage and causing anger.

As I said before, sometimes avoidance is the right thing, because the setting isn't right for a discussion or there are other people nearby who would not benefit from it.

There is a time and a place to strip off the Fig Leaf of Complacency and speak up, but we must be discerning.

Just because we have the right to broadcast our opinions doesn't mean we must exercise that right wherever and whenever.

In closing this chapter I'll share this: Just the work of writing this section—saying what was on my heart about this tough subject—opened my Fig Leaf Closet door. That Complacency leaf is now shredded and in the trash bin.

I hope it stays there.

Questions for Personal Reflection

1. Do you tend to shy away from controversial subjects in conversation with others, or do you dive right in and let the chips fall where they may?

   _____

   _____

   _____

   _____

2. In your own life, are there people, settings, or subjects in which you avoid confrontational conversation?

   _____

   _____

   _____

   _____

3. Is there anyone in your life with whom a disagreement over deeply held beliefs has led to the destruction of the relationship? What can you do to repair that relationship?

   _____

   _____

   _____

   _____

Simon Peter said to them, "I am going fishing."
John 21:3

The Fig Leaf of
HIDING BEHIND FAILURE

I'll be honest with you.

I don't want to write this chapter. I'm pretty sure I don't have to explain myself, right?

Who in their right mind likes to fail? I sure don't, but I have a lot of experience at it, as I'm sure everyone on the planet has.

We can all come up with examples of how we have failed in business, in our families, in simply doing life. Let's talk about that Fig Leaf of Failure and how that one fits us. It might be the tightest one of all, even more so than Fear. In fact, failure begets fear, and interestingly enough, the reverse is true also. They're partners, twin demons sent by the Enemy to defeat us.

But God knows our Enemy in ways we can't, and He can take those devilish twins and turn them on their heads . . . if we allow Him.

How do we hide behind failure? Let's get down to it.

Failure means I failed in some way. *Elementary, my dear Watson*, you say.

- I said that harsh word and turned someone away from friendship with God.

- I neglected my parent, my child, my spouse, or my friend. I paid no attention to their need, intent only on my own.

- I got fired from a job.

- I got a divorce.

- My child cut me off and won't speak to me. (Ouch, this is getting painful . . .)

- I cussed.

- I tried something new and it flopped—big time. So big, it seems like people are laughing at me.

- I forgot—a date, a birthday, a promise, a commitment.

So moving down this list, and maybe adding your own failures along the way, it's getting pretty heavy, isn't it?

When I typed the last word of that list, I felt like I was buried under a ten-foot-high pile of garbage. I could even smell it—rancid, rotten failure upon failure. I'm depressing myself just reading back over the list, thinking about the refuse of mistakes I may have buried other people under.

And thinking about the failures I didn't list.

Yeah, there's more. But I think we have enough to go with.

But back to hiding . . . wearing the Fig Leaf of Failure. Why do we zoom to the closet door and grab that sketchy leaf and wrap it around us?

Maybe the reason is different for everyone, but here's what I came up with for myself:

> I hide behind failure because if I don't—if I let my failure out, examine it—I might have to try again. And fail again. No, I don't want to go there again. I might run out of leaves to wear.

That's it. That's why I'd rather hide, because the pain of failure isn't that everyone knows about it, that they might call me a loser, a no-talent girl who fancies herself a writer, a singer, a mom—it's that I might have to go through it again.

What can I do? Quit?

Taking myself out of the game is an option, but sadly, not a good one.

Just ask Peter. Yeah, the *apostle* Peter.

Big fisherman inside the inner circle of Jesus, spokesperson for the other eleven. The mouthpiece who stood up in Acts 2 and bravely gave his first sermon. But where was he just before that? Maybe about fifty or so days before that?

There's no getting around it—he was running, his fisherman's sandals slapping the hard dirt, arms flailing, robes flying.

But hidden underneath those robes? Yep, you guessed it . . . fig leaves.

After the kiss of Judas on Jesus's cheek and after Peter whacked off the ear of a poor schmuck named Malchus, Peter hightailed it out of the garden, leaving his Master to the mercy of the Jewish authorities and Roman soldiers.

He didn't go home though. He lurked and skulked around the high priest's courtyard to see what would happen next.

And what happened next sent big Peter down a tiny rabbit hole of hiding.

Three denials and a rooster crow later, he couldn't escape that soul-piercing stare of Jesus. The stare that blared the question, *What are you doing here, Simon Peter?*

Peter had no answer.

But then his story took a different turn.

After Jesus was raised from the dead, even after Peter had seen Him with his own eyes and touched His resurrected body, Peter hid again. He decided to go back to what he knew, to what he was good at. Back to same old same old.

He was stuck in his betrayal of Jesus, unable to move past it. I know. I've been there.

I can almost hear his thoughts. *I'm no good at being an apostle. I not only denied Jesus once, but three times, for crying out loud. But at least I can catch fish!*

So off the big apostle went to the shore, to his boat and the nets he'd grown up with. No more of this preaching stuff, no more wandering around with the most loved and hated man who'd ever lived, thank you very much.

But you know what? Just like God found Jonah in the gut of a fish, He saw Peter, right through him actually, and tenderly put him back in the game.

It wasn't long before Acts 2 happened and the revival began, all because Peter took a hard look at his failure and stripped off the fig leaf hanging in tatters around him.

Peter allowed God to reclothe him with robes that would never wear out.

It's been said that failure means you tried . . . and that's *all* it is. The human who never fails has never tried.

We mustn't let failure, or the fear of it, sideline us in this life. Whatever God has given you (and me) to do, we must allow Him to equip us to do it. It doesn't matter what it is—to travel across the world or across the street to meet a need, write a book or a song, make quilts for the homeless, or lead a committee in the local church.

We must examine what we are passionate about, pray fervently for direction, then leap into the unknown. And if we fail, remember: it's only failure if we fail to get up again.

Questions for Personal Reflection

1. If you had to choose, what would you say is your biggest failure in life thus far?

   _____

   _____

   _____

   _____

2. How has that failure defined your life? Do you view that failure as unredeemable?

   _____

   _____

   _____

   _____

3. If you could, would you go back to that failure and make a different choice? Or will you allow God to continue to redeem your failure and thank Him for how He has used it and is still using it to showcase His grace to you and to others?

   _____

   _____

   _____

   _____

The Pharisee stood and prayed thus with himself,
"God, I thank You that I am not like other men."
Luke 18:11

The Fig Leaf of

HIDING BEHIND SELF SUFFICIENCY

The Pharisee in the verse above spent time in prayer. That's good, right? But his prayer was all about how he'd done this, he'd done that, and how he wasn't like the filthy tax collector standing in the back of the room. The Pharisee gave God a list of reasons why God should accept him. And did you catch the words, "prayed thus *with himself*"? I laugh every time I read it.

As we do.

I can do it myself!

Ever heard those words from a child? You step back and watch as the little tyke tries and tries to do it herself. Fix a Lego structure, tie the shoe, get the toothpaste on the toothbrush. You wait patiently as she fumbles the shiny barrette, drops it, and finally gives up with a stamp of her tiny sneakered foot.

Or do you hear those words careening out of your own mouth?

Racing into the building for a job interview, you send a gimmee prayer up to God Almighty because you neglected to ask in the days leading up to this one—you were just too busy.

Please help me get this job, God, You know I need it. Translation: *I know I'm unqualified for this job, but can You just give me an edge for old times' sake?*

I take the platform, pick up the mic, and listen for the music to cue me. During that thirty seconds, I pray for God's blessing on the song *I* chose, the one that showcases *my* talent, and the one *I* decided this audience needed to hear. *God, please bless* me *as* I *sing. Help* me *not to make any mistakes, and may the people listen to* me. Translation: *I'm a good vocalist. If You will help me to not embarrass myself, I'll give You the glory.*

Self-sufficiency. Oh, how it gets me into trouble!

How about you?

Ever said, with me, *I can do it myself, God*?

Of course, we don't say it that way. Sometimes we don't even use words—by our actions we declare our independence from our Creator.

We refuse to bathe every moment of our humdrum day in prayer. If there's nothing big going on, nothing to scare us, we don't have to leave the house today, no sickness or financial loss looming, our children—of whatever age—are behaving themselves, the neighbors aren't annoying us, and our churches are full every Sunday, what need have we to bring to God?

We can get along just fine, thank you very much—until we can't.

Until cancer rears its ugly head.

Until the stock market flips a downturn.

Until the words, *I want a divorce* launch into the room.

Until that beloved family member says "never contact me again."

Until you hear, "You're fired—clean out your desk and go home."

Then without warning, the truth crashes upon the rocky shore of my life—I need Him every second of every day of every month, 24/7/365.

Without Him I'm a fish out water. I'm as helpless as a bug under a shoe. And I'm as answerless as the baby born yesterday.

Self-sufficiency is a disease. One that rots me from the inside out, consumes my relationship with the lover of my soul until there's nothing left . . . nothing left but me.

The me who can do nothing but gasp for air, squirm under the shoe, and flail my arms and cry.

I choose God-sufficiency today. I'm sick of self.

How about you?

Questions for Personal Reflection

1. Are you a can-do type—you're willing to tackle anything? How do you fit God into that picture?

    _____
    _____
    _____
    _____

2. Share a personal story of self-sufficiency becoming self-*in*sufficiency.

    _____
    _____
    _____
    _____

3. How will you flip your circumstance on its head so that God is celebrated as sufficient for it—and not you?

    _____

    _____

    _____

    _____

*If a brother or sister is naked and destitute of daily
food, and one of you says to them, "Depart in peace,
be warmed and filled," but you do not give them
the things which are needed for the body,
what does it profit?*
James 2:15–16

The Fig Leaf of

HIDING *BEHIND* PRAYER . . . OR HIDING *FROM* PRAYER

W hy both?
Because we wear both. At least I do.

How many times have we listened to a friend's grief or worry or heard about their need of food, money, transportation, and said, "I will pray for you"?

There's nothing wrong with praying for the needs of others, mind you, but in James we learn that God expects so much more from us.

If we pray for the need to be met, that's all well and good, but what if—just what if—*you* are God's answer to that prayer, hmm?

James says if we have the means to help—whether a ride to a doctor appointment or grocery store, paying a bill, or sitting over a cup of coffee and just lending your ear—and we don't, then we probably should not bother praying either.

Sound harsh? Maybe. But think of it this way.

If *you* are God's answer to your friend's prayer, and you choose not to be that answer, you negate your own prayer for your friend. Do we really think God will answer our prayer if we refuse to obey Him?

The Fig Leaf of Hiding Behind Prayer hangs in the section of my closet labeled *Hypocrisy*. Hypocrisy is saying one thing and doing another. The apostle James was all over that, believe me. It's easier to say, with a smile and a quick pat on the shoulder, "I'll pray for you," instead of going the extra mile with tangible help.

To only offer prayer when I have the means to offer myself is the height of hypocrisy.

Besides that, if I'm honest with myself, I have to admit that by the time I've arrived home I've forgotten half of what was going on with my friend, and by the next day, I've forgotten to pray. If I'd actually provided that tangible help, I'd probably not forget to pray either.

On the flip side of all that is the Fig Leaf of Hiding from Prayer. That's a little more subtle.

I'm a busy person. Even though I'm "retired" I still have a daily schedule I keep. It's home is right next to my laptop so I don't forget anything. When I had a job outside my home, I didn't need a daily schedule next to my computer—I had a boss whose job was to make sure I did mine.

Busyness, though, can strip me of the desire and the energy to pray. In fact, sometimes I'd rather do anything rather than pray—it's hard work. It's the opposite of Hiding Behind Prayer.

There doesn't seem to be the same sense of accomplishment when I spend fifteen minutes in prayer as when I spend the same amount of time creating sentences in this book, or scheduling social media posts, or answering emails.

How did I get to the place where time spent in doing seems more productive than time spent in conversation with my Lord at the foot of His throne?

What could happen in my little corner of the world if I placed a premium on prayer time over laptop time?

That question reminds me of two sisters, Martha and Mary, who were close friends with Jesus when His feet walked this earth. The sisters couldn't have been more different.

Martha had the gift of hospitality. She loved company, especially Jesus and His disciples.

One day Martha was up to her eyeballs in preparing food for their guests, making sure everything was clean and inviting and that everyone was comfortable. In a word, she was harried. And disgruntled when she looked into the next room and saw Mary sitting idly at the feet of Jesus.

What did she do? What I would've done, and maybe you also.

She marched in and complained to the God of the universe that Mary wasn't helping her and please make her get busy.

Jesus tenderly admonished her. He told her in so many words that Mary had chosen the better part, and Martha would do well to do the same.

Discussion over.

Sitting quietly at the feet of Jesus, hearing Him speak, letting His words sink in, making requests—all of this is vastly more important than *doing*. Difficult, but more important.

Why do I say it's difficult?

Because *doing* glorifies me.

Being glorifies Him.

So both sides of this coin are wrong—Hiding *Behind* Prayer and Hiding *From* Prayer.

The key is to *pray* for direction before *doing*, and if God says *I'm* the answer to the prayer, then I must not shirk. Someone else's faith might be on the line.

The real deal, the holy place God wants us to get to, is Hiding *in* Prayer.

After I let that sink in, I have an assignment—for both of us: to go strip out the *Hypocrisy* side of our closets and vow never to wear those fig leaves again.

Questions for Personal Reflection

1. When your friend or loved one asks you to pray, is it your normal practice to say, "Okay, I will pray for you"? Or do you stop what you're doing and pray right then, either in person, in a text, or on the phone?

    _____

    _____

    _____

    _____

2. What is your hypocrisy quotient? Do you say you'll *pray* for the need when you actually have the means to *provide* for the need?

    _____

    _____

    _____

    _____

3. Would you rather *do* (like Martha) than *pray* (like Mary)? Be honest—whom are you glorifying with regard to your answer?

    _____

    _____

    _____

    _____

He was oppressed and He was afflicted,
Yet He opened not His mouth . . .
Isaiah 53:7

The Fig Leaf of

HIDING BEHIND RIGHTS

I might be in serious trouble with this one. *Rights* is one of those topics sure to make someone's blood boil. I see the hot button flashing, fingers poised over it.

The thing is though, everyone has them. *Rights*, I mean. Determining where mine end and yours begin is the part that gets us all in a lather.

Some believe our rights are God given—there is plenty of evidence in the Scriptures for that viewpoint. For example, the right to worship Him—as He pleases though, not as I please.

But some rights are not spelled out in His Word. Some rights—to the great displeasure of a few, I'm certain—are bestowed by governments. For instance, the right to own property, to seek employment, to vote. These aren't enumerated in the Scriptures, but they do follow the spirit of God-given rights.

So what's the problem?

As I said at the beginning, determining where my rights end and yours begin is the thorny path over which we must tread.

We tend to cling to our rights, don't we? Like a bag of M&M's, we pour them out, pile them up, sort them, and refuse to share. Even with the starving person next to us.

They're *mine*.

What would it take for us to loosen our grip on a dearly valued right? And why would we do that? So that another person can enjoy his or her right. What do I mean?

Let's talk about one of those hot-button rights to which we cling.

The right to free speech. Yeah, that one. I'd like everyone to remove your finger from where it's poised over that hot button and back away. Let's examine this right before we all jam our fingers down and create a free-for-all.

Free speech—what does it mean?

That we can say anything we want with impunity? That it doesn't matter what we say in the public square, or how we say it, because freedom of speech is part of our DNA?

Some folks believe just that. If they hold an opinion about anything under the sun, they blare it forth without consequence because they have a right to.

Not all speech is protected. We've all heard that yelling *Fire!* in a crowded theater when there is no fire is not protected speech and can have serious consequences.

It's true, though, that stating your opinion is protected

speech in America. And you can state your opinion in any setting, using any words you choose.

When I was a child, though, not so much. Varying opinions were encouraged by my parents, but we had to observe two rules: say it with respect, and back it up with facts.

So when does stating my opinion on a matter, whether a large or a small one, become Hiding Behind Rights?

Good question.

Discernment is the order of the day when it comes to clinging to our rights.

What if I'm at a school board meeting and I gain the microphone? I do have every right to make my voice heard on whatever topic is under discussion. And so do you. My language should be forceful, but polite and civil, in order to get my point across. And I should be prepared, so as not to hop off down a bunny trail and waste time.

But what if I'm at a family gathering and the same topic comes up? One of those divisive topics that can derail the pleasure of family fellowship with just one sentence? I daresay that most of the time, those topics arise in that kind setting without warning, so preparedness is out the window.

Do I have the right to make my voice heard? Absolutely.

But should I? Only I can decide that. Just because I *can* say a thing doesn't mean I *should* say a thing.

My decision should be based upon additional factors other than the right to be heard.

What are those factors? Glad you asked.

- Who is sitting around the table? Children? Some topics should be discussed by adults out of the hearing of children—especially those subjects that cause rising emotion.

- What is the occasion? A birthday? An anniversary? A holiday? Those celebrations are few and far between for most of us. Why muddy the waters with an emotional back-and-forth that likely will not change anyone's mind? I guarantee you that months and years down the road, that contentious atmosphere will be all anyone remembers about what should've been a happy occasion.

- And what is the mindset of your family members and friends on this topic, which has just blown into the room without warning? Do you even know?

There are probably more factors we could add to this list, and it will vary with each of us.

As stated earlier, discernment is the order of the day when deciding to speak up or keep silent. There is a time and a place for discussion, for exercising our right to free speech, and we must be prepared to know which setting we are in.

We have only touched on the exercise of free speech, but the same process can be applied to any of the rights we try to hide behind.

If we just blithely go about our lives, exercising our rights with much abandon and zero discernment, we could be denying the rights of others. We wouldn't deliberately choose to be safe in our person and our home if exercising that right would deny our neighbor the same . . . would we?

In order to get this whole rights thing right, it takes thought as well as placing others in the position of being more important than ourselves.

We need look no further than Jesus for a prime example of getting it right. For a time, He gave up His deity and His right to live in heaven with His Father so that you and I could experience eternal life with Him—and not eternal death without Him.

Jesus put us first—we must do no less for those He puts in our lives.

The Fig Leaf of Hiding Behind Rights must go.

I'm on my way to my closet now. You?

Questions for Personal Reflection

1. Out of all the personal freedoms and rights you enjoy, what single right do you cling to? That one right where you draw the line in the sand?

   _____

   _____

   _____

   _____

2. Under what circumstances would you be willing to give up that right?

   _____

   _____

   _____

   _____

3. How important is it to you to safeguard the rights of others? How far are you willing to go to accomplish that?

   _____

   _____

   _____

   _____

. . . lest any root of bitterness springing up cause
trouble, and by this many become defiled . . .
Hebrews 12:15

The Fig Leaf of
HIDING BEHIND ANGER

We all get mad.

We should get mad over some things.

Injustice. Children harmed. Lawlessness. Governments out of control. War.

But when does righteous anger become the Fig Leaf of Hiding Behind Anger?

Think of the last time you became angry. Really angry.

Maybe you got fired for no good reason. Maybe you accidently discovered your spouse's indiscretion. Maybe your teenager's school principal called and told you your child has been skipping school, or that she had been caught stealing, or that he was dealing drugs.

Your anger meter shoots up and beyond the stratosphere.

But, you say, these are things that should make me angry, right?

Yes. Absolutely. But the next question is the key to knowing if you're Hiding Behind Anger: What did you do with your anger, and how long did you remain angry?

Sorry. That's two questions.

There's a verse in Scripture that mentions not letting the sun go down on our anger. Now, that doesn't mean that the next day we go about our business, choosing to forget about what made us angry. That we can't acknowledge our hurt and disappointment twenty-four hours later.

No, that verse means we must channel that anger in a different direction.

Up, not inward or outward.

If I channel my anger—say, at another driver who cuts me off—inward or outward instead of upward, two things will happen. Two things that are absolutely not helpful to me.

The inward channel results in hypersensitivity to what other drivers do on the road . . . as if I've never done something stupid when driving. It causes me to watch what others do and pick apart their driving choices. (Can you tell this is personal for me, that this is confession time?)

If I channel my anger inwardly, I could cause an accident because I'm paying too much attention to the "sins" of others instead of focusing on my own.

Ouch!

Also, letting my anger stay and float down that inward channel, especially if the emotion is caused by something more serious than being cut off in traffic, will cause all kinds of repercussions later.

If I get fired for no discernible reason and I channel that anger inwardly, I may end up with physical symptoms, like an ulcer.

Channeling anger outward causes other consequences.

I might try to publicize what was done to me, talk about it everywhere in different settings, calling out whoever fired me. And what's wrong with that? you might ask. People should know how that company treats its employees, right? Aren't we responsible to protect others from such a company? To make sure the next employee doesn't experience the same?

Maybe. I'm going to take a stab in the dark, though, and say that protecting others is probably not my primary motivation. And I'd be right. Motive is everything.

Here's the most important consequence of channeling anger outwardly: my indiscriminate, angry, accusatory words—while they may be justified—will most likely make me look bad and will certainly tarnish the reputation of the Christ I claim.

We all know someone who has allowed anger to be the defining emotion in their life. Think about that person for a moment.

Anger doesn't just come out of that person's mouth—it exudes from her pores. Every endeavor is tainted by anger. Decisions, big or small, are skewed and skewered by anger. And some of those decisions are life changing, can never be re-decided. That person's anger determines the course of her life. Left unchecked it will most certainly flow into the next generation.

The Fig Leaf of Hiding Behind Anger is a bit different from all the other fig leaves in my closet. How so?

It's never suffered in private. Even though I think I'm hiding behind it, my anger flaunts itself like a diva in a sparkly dress so everyone can see it for what it is.

It never stays in the closet—even if I lock the door and throw away the key. If I don't do the hard work of facing my anger and doing battle with it, it will find a way out and cling to me like a leech, sucking away the blood and the life God wants to give me. And sadly, infecting others.

This fig leaf might be the hardest of all to rid myself of. It might take the rest of my life.

But with God's help, I plan to try. How about you? Let's go to war together, shall we?

Questions for Personal Reflection

1. With whom are you angry today? Share the circumstances briefly.

   _____

   _____

   _____

   _____

2. Has you anger affected anyone else in your circle of family and friends? Share honestly about how your anger has affected you.

   _____

   _____

   _____

   _____

3. What steps can you take immediately, and over time, that will not only dissipate your anger but heal it? And would you be willing to encourage others to do likewise?

   _____

   _____

   _____

   _____

Go therefore and make disciples of all the nations.
Matthew 28:19

The Fig Leaf of
HIDING BEHIND MY PASTOR

I'm confident that most pastors will give two thumbs-up for this chapter. I know mine would.

This'll be a short section—because it's not hard to figure out what we're doing when we invite someone to church but never mention Jesus in conversation with that someone, right?

It's my job to invite my friend to church. It's the pastor's job to tell my friend about Jesus.

The problem with that is . . . it's wrongheaded, according to the Scriptures—and most pastors, I might add.

Jesus was clear in Matthew 28: *Go therefore . . .*

Who was He talking to? Just the disciples who were present that day? Just pastors and priests? Someone else?

Umm . . . no. He spoke to us, gave us our marching orders.

His disciples watched expectantly as He spread His arms and began His last sermon on Earth.

Maybe they thought He'd give them a bullet-point list of how to go about defeating the hated Romans. Or tips on how to raise the dead and cure the sick after His feet left the ground. Or maybe even how to find the right spouse, how to create a killer sermon, how to catch the most fish.

Nope!

His last sermon to His followers had nothing to do with any of that. He had something much more vital on His mind.

Don't become a behind-the-pastor hider.

He wanted all His followers to be good news proclaimers.

My pastor is fond of saying to his people that he couldn't possibly go to all of our friends, relatives, and neighbors with the gospel—"I'm only one person. You are many."

So, my friends, lurking in the shadows behind our pastors just won't do anymore, will it? We must go and spread the God-is-love news ourselves to the people He has placed in our paths.

Just inviting them to church isn't enough. It's a start, but not the whole enchilada, by any means. How about lunch afterward, which we pay for, to discuss the sermon? Leave the door open for an honest conversation about what it meant to them.

If we all did this, think how full our churches could be and how rested our pastors might be. Sounds like a win-win to me.

In my mind's eye, I see my pastor handing me the shears to cut my Hiding Behind My Pastor Fig Leaf to ribbons.

Your pastor is right behind mine.

Questions for Personal Reflection

1. How often do you just invite someone to church without having laid any groundwork—expecting your pastor to "fill in the gaps"?

   _____

   _____

   _____

   _____

2. How can you change that approach? Think of some ways you can encourage your unbelieving friend or loved one *before* extending the invitation to attend church.

   _____

   _____

   _____

   _____

3. Are you willing to talk to your believing friends and loved ones about this and encourage them to "go therefore ..."?

   _____

   _____

   _____

   _____

So Judas threw the money into the temple and left.
Then he went away and hanged himself.
Matthew 27:5

The Fig Leaf of
HIDING BEHIND MY PLAN

I am a planner. I start planning dinner for Monday night on Saturday. And sometimes I cook dinner at eight in the morning. Why?

Because that's my plan.

I visit my father at his facility across town three to four days a week. Why?

Because that's my plan. I hate letting go of a plan. Plans ground me, give me a direction to go. That's not a bad thing, but sometimes . . .

Sometimes God taps me on the shoulder and says *Let's talk, Deb.*

About what? I say, eyes focused on the daily schedule I keep next to my laptop.

About your plan, right there under your pen. It needs adjustment.

Why? I grip my pen harder.

Because that plan is not My plan—it's yours. Let Me tell you about what I want you to do today . . .

And so it goes. My plan—right out the window . . . if I'm smart, that is. It's never smart to cling to my plan tighter than the one given to me by Him.

Have you ever had a conversation like that?

Nehemiah was a man with a plan. Remember him? The cupbearer to the king. And believe me, that job took some guts. He never knew whether today's taste of the king's grog would put him writhing on the floor or not.

Then out of the blue, God gave him another plan—maybe a much more dangerous and complicated one. He received word, in his digs in Persia, that the wall in Jerusalem was broken down and had become a laughingstock to the whole world. That broke Nehemiah's heart. He began a conversation with God about it, and God gave him his marching orders.

Into the fray he went, supervising the rebuilding of the wall while fending off criticism, ridicule, and the enemies of Israel, who were intent on destroying God's people.

Nehemiah had a plan, but God's was better. Instead of protecting the life of the Persian king, he was sent to preserve the nation of Israel.

There's another story straight from the Scriptures that should give us even greater pause about gripping that self-made plan. I'm talking about a guy named Judas.

He had a plan—no less than the overthrow of the Roman government and the freedom of the Holy Land. Sounds like a good plan, right? The Romans were cruel taskmasters back in the day, and there were many Judases meeting in secret to work out a plot for insurrection.

But the plan Judas devised had one tiny flaw. He wanted to use Messiah as the front man and install Him as king once the Romans had been dispatched. Harebrained scheme, right? The God of the universe a puppet of some religious zealots?

The unraveling of Judas's plan began at the Last Supper, when Jesus looked him in the eye and told him to get on with it.

Of course Jesus knew the plan—He's God. So Judas left the supper and got on with it.

His plan fell apart when his conscience got busy and he experienced an uncustomary feeling—remorse. He tried to return those thirty pieces of silver and was run out of town on a rail . . . so to speak. Judas, in his bitter state of mind, did the only thing left. He hung himself.

Whew! Do I want to go to those lengths to hang on to my measly plan? I think not.

I'll admit, my daily schedule probably doesn't carry the weight of these two examples, but who am I to say that it doesn't?

My yesterday's schedule looked like this:

- Bible reading—Deuteronomy chapters 1–3.
- Write 1,000 words on my current project (this manuscript, by the way).
- Write an Amazon review of a book I'm reading.
- Review Blog Tour information and send in.
- Review NCWA book launch information.
- Haircut with Heather at 11:00 a.m.
- Go to the store.
- Go see Dad.
- Return home and veg out.

Nothing even close to traveling to another country to supervise wall building. Or negotiating with an enemy government with the intent to overthrow said enemy government.

No, this is just the mundane plan of an author with several irons in the fire.

But if I look closely at it, there are a couple of tasks that *could* lead to a conversation about God to someone. I must always count on God to lead me to those conversations in the midst of my plan's mundaneness.

And I should, without a doubt, be ready to scrap the whole thing if God has a different assignment for me.

On some days, for a confirmed planner like myself, it would take a Herculean effort to peel off the Fig Leaf of Hiding Behind My Plan and go with God's.

How about you?

Questions for Personal Reflection

1. Are you a meticulous planner or a confirmed winger? We know what a planner looks like—what does winging your day look like? Are there any drawbacks you can think of to being a *no-plan, no-how* follower of Jesus?

    _____
    _____
    _____
    _____

2. If you're a planner, do you become frothy if your carefully scheduled day gets scrapped by someone (or Someone) other than yourself? What do you think is the cause of that froth?

    _____
    _____
    _____

————————————————————————————

3. Do you think it's better to be a combo planner/winger? What would that look like?

    ————————————————————————
    ————————————————————————
    ————————————————————————
    ————————————————————————

*They found fault. For the Pharisees and all the Jews
do not eat unless they wash their hands in a special
way, holding the tradition of the elders.*
Mark 7:2–3

19

The Fig Leaf of
HIDING BEHIND TRADITION

I have served on several teams and committees in churches and workplaces. There's one concept that almost always
rears its head in one way or another when ideas are kicked
around in meetings.

Know what it is?

But we've always done it that way!

That pronouncement should have its own line item in any
meeting agenda, but it should look like this:

But we've always done it that way!

Tradition. Hiding behind the way we've always done it. It's
one of those concepts that can kill or create. What do I mean
by that?

Let's take a bunny trail back in time about two thousand or so years, to when Jesus walked barefoot on the earth. He was the best tradition buster on the planet in His day.

- Don't talk to Samaritans.

- Don't talk to women.

- Wash your hands this way, not that way.

- You can bring this sacrifice on this day, but you must bring a different one tomorrow.

- You can help that old guy who stumbled and fell out in the street today, but woe to you if you help him up tomorrow.

We could probably fill the rest of the pages in this book with the list of the traditions (translation: rules) that the religious leaders made the people follow back then.

Some of those rules came right out of God's lawbook, like the ones about sacrifices—but others sprang right from the selfish minds of those religious folks who had nothing but control of the masses on their minds.

Don't get me wrong. Many traditions we keep are good and necessary.

Some that come to mind are birthdays, anniversaries, prayer first thing in the morning, daily Bible reading, baptism, communion, Christmas (to remind us of the birth of Jesus, *not* the guy all dressed in red fur scouting the landscape for chimneys), Easter (to celebrate the resurrection of Jesus, *not* His floppy-eared creation clutching a basket of goodies), and many, many more. Some traditions are unique to each family, and others are celebrated by millions around the world.

But there are those pesky traditions that instead of leading us into the mercy and grace of God, drag us into a different arena.

The arena of one-upmanship. That place where we say to each other, as the Pharisees, Sadducees, and those other *cees* did in Jesus's day:

- See what I did? No one has ever donated a new cross for our church before . . .

- Look how much I put in the offering plate today!

- Look how that woman is dressed . . . in church even!

- Hey, you can't come to this service. It's communion— only for believers.

- Here, you sit in the back pew. Front pews are reserved for members in good standing.

Maybe your church or group never ventures into this arena. Good for you if you don't. But I'm afraid these scenarios, and many more, are all too familiar among those of us who claim to be Christians.

We must examine our *we've always done it this way* mindset. We must critique which arena we're living in.

Look around. Are your traditions producing glad hearts and holiness, fellowship and communion? Or are you standing in the dirt surrounded by other gladiators, ready to spring on one another and grind one another down?

And what about the cheering crowds in your arena?

Are they comprised of the great cloud of witnesses spoken of in Hebrews 12, surrounding us and cheering us on to finish our race? Or is your crowd a mob of bloodthirsty folks who thrive more on the failures of others than on their successes?

Instead, God calls us to hold on to the good, holy practices and celebrations, those which lead our families, friends, and coworkers into the arena of mercy and grace, the creativity of a good God who continually holds out His hand of forgiveness to all who will receive it.

That Fig Leaf of Tradition. Let's rid ourselves of it once and for all, replacing it with His robes of righteousness—today, before it's too late.

Questions for Personal Reflection

1. Are there any traditions in your Fig Leaf Closet that you hide behind? Those traditions that give you warm, fuzzy feelings—that all is well, you've done everything you can to measure up?

    _____

    _____

    _____

    _____

2. What traditions should you hold on to?

    _____

    _____

    _____

    _____

3. How many traditions do you follow that lead you and others to worship *God* instead of worshiping *yourself* for how perfectly you've performed? Make a new list of those you do or would like to do that lead others to worship God.

    _____

    _____

    _____

    _____

*That very day Pilate and Herod became friends
with each other, for previously they had been at
enmity with each other.*
Luke 23:12

20

The Fig Leaf of
HIDING BEHIND POLITICS

P olitics. It's been around since forever. In the verse above,
we see the problem with it. Pilate, a Roman, and Herod,
a Jew—previously enemies in every sense of the word—laid
aside their cultural and political differences to achieve a common goal: to get rid of that pesky itinerant preacher who chal-
lenged their authority.

Politics is most likely a subject no one wants to talk about.
However, I think we must, given the current climate of our culture.

What is the first thing you think about over your first cup
of coffee or tea or water in the morning?

I'll speak up. I think about the worries I have on my mind
regarding the chaos in the world, how our elected officials seem

to make decisions over our heads that affect us adversely (and they don't seem to care), and how there seems to be thousands of people all over the globe who have turned their backs on faith, traditional family values, and God Himself.

How depressing is it to start my day like that, right?

But on the flip side . . .

Is there a place for politics in our daily lives? Absolutely. But we must figure out where that place is and keep politics in its place.

I've heard some say that when they wake up, they have so disciplined themselves that their first thoughts are directed heavenward, toward God's throne. Their first prayer of the morning is *God, what do you want me to do today?*

I like that.

Much better than, with a firm grip on my coffee cup, I say to my husband, "Did you hear about _____? How dare they do that. What is this world coming to?"

You get the idea.

I start my day by dwelling on the evil running rampant on this planet instead of upon the sovereign Lord of the universe, my Creator, who at some point will flick His little finger at the mess we've made, destroying anything and everything that is not of Him.

Recently, I've examined my Fig Leaf of Hiding Behind Politics and discovered a dismaying truth.

While I'm wearing it snugly wrapped around my heart and my mind, the truth of God and His Word disappears.

What do I mean?

Just this: while I'm wearing that worn-out, filthy fig leaf, there's no room for anything else. That fig leaf has the power— power *I've* given it—to drown out God's voice of peace, to nullify the Scriptures I've memorized, and to pierce the armor of trust He makes available to me.

Yeah, that armor is still wrapped around my chest—but hidden under the Fig Leaf of Politics—and now the Enemy has the ability to pierce that armor with the arrow of fear.

Oy!

I must uncover that armor of trust, gaze at it, meditate upon the truth I find in His Word—and then rip the Fig Leaf of Politics to shreds and throw it on the trash heap called Lies and Deception.

We've had a little fun with this chapter, visualizing and naming the thought processes that lead us to despondency over the global morass in which we live, right?

But the fun we've had must not deter us from the path our God wants us to walk—the path that leads to His side—as we navigate the crooked roads built by mankind.

Let's get off those crooked roads and place our feet on the straight path that He has made for us—the one that leads to Him first thing in the morning, shall we?

I'm there.

Questions for Personal Reflection

1. Politics—love it or hate it? Do you enjoy a good debate, or would you rather chew a rock?

   _____

   _____

   _____

   _____

2. What is your first thought most mornings? *How did we get here?* Or, *God where do You want me today?*

   _____

   _____

----

3. How can you accomplish that mental shift so that your first thoughts are heavenward?

----

*Let no one despise your youth, but be an example to
the believers in word, in conduct, in love, in spirit,
in faith, in purity.*
1 Timothy 4:12

The Fig Leaf of
HIDING BEHIND AGE

I hate to bring this up, but we aren't getting any younger. At
least, I'm not.

The Fig Leaf of Hiding Behind Age is rather tricky.

Meaning: *I'm too young for* _____, *which God is calling me to do.* Or, *I'm too old for* _____, *which
God is calling me to do.* (Fill in the blank with the mission God
has given you to complete.)

It could go either way, sometimes both ways, depending on
your age, dear reader.

Remember the apostle John? Lived into his nineties and he
still listened to God and penned the portions of Scripture God
told him to write.

I'm getting to the point where it's definitely *I'm too old to be jumping out of my comfort zone into* that, *God. Really? Did you forget I was born in 19**?* I say *that* to my Creator as I'm pulling out my fig leaf for the day, completely discounting the fact that He was actually there the day of my conception, the day I started grade school, the day I graduated, got married, had my first, second, and third child . . . Need I go on?

And, oh, He's in my office with me right now, watching and cheering me on as my fingers fly over the laptop keys saying how old I am. Sheesh! You'd think I would've learned something in the last umpteen decades, like

- age is just a number;
- when God gives an assignment, He doesn't say, *Deb, if you're feeling up to it, if you're not too tired or feeling too old, if you've had enough coffee, here's what I want you to do;*
- when God gives an assignment, He moves me out of my zone, encourages me, and equips me in ways I can't possibly envision ahead of time;
- all those verses in His Word that promise He is with me wherever I go, He will guide my footsteps, and He will be with me until the end of the age and throughout eternity . . . He means it.

You'd think I would've soaked some of that up.

But maybe you're on the flip side of the age coin.

Ever wonder if you're too young to do what God wants you to do? Too young to give up a career and go in a different direction? To pass on making a lot of money until you've made your mark, until you've reached a certain financial level?

God couldn't possibly want you to skip financial security in favor of financial uncertainty, right? Especially in the markets we suffer through today.

It's something to think about.

It certainly makes much more sense to build up your savings while you're young and *then* move out into the mission God gives you. After all, if you have a big bank account, you won't need to rely on donors to your cause. You can fund the whole venture, right? Makes sense.

Not quite. God's sense of *making sense* is as different from ours as night and day.

You see, if we are able to do it ourselves, then what need have we to rely on God? Uh-oh, time out here. Do you see the problem?

The problem, once again, is self-effort, which is a definite no-no in serving God in the arena to which He calls us.

So whether we wear that pesky Fig Leaf of Hiding Behind Age because we think we're too old or too young, it's a problem either way.

Time to put *that* fig leaf in the yard sale, take it to the landfill, or cut it up and use it for fertilizer in my garden.

Wait—I don't have a garden. And I'm too old to start one now.

You with me?

Questions for Personal Reflection

1. Ever wonder if you're too old or too young to be doing what you're doing? Ever give God the what-for when He places you on that next path? It's okay—you can be honest on this page.

    _____
    _____
    _____
    _____

2. An Elisabeth Elliot quote fits right here: "Sometimes fear does not subside and one must choose to do it afraid."[1] What is God asking you to do that you think you're too old or too young to do?

_____

_____

_____

_____

3. What decision will you make today regarding serving God no matter what age you are?

_____

_____

_____

_____

---

1   https://www.kylewinkler.org/articles/the-secret-to-con-quering-everything-youre-afraid-to-do/.

*The young man said to Him, "All these things I have
kept from my youth. What do I still lack?"*
Matthew 19:20

The Fig Leaf of
HIDING BEHIND
ACCOMPLISHMENTS

W hat do I still lack? Indeed.

Let's face it, folks. We often derive our perceived value to the world by what we've accomplished. My Fig Leaf of Hiding Behind Accomplishments might look something like this:

- I graduated from high school.

- I got married.

- I birthed three children and have four stepchildren, who are doing well in their own lives.

- I had a career of thirty-plus years in a field I enjoyed.

- I was a vocalist from age fifteen and enjoyed singing in

groups and soloing before audiences in churches and other venues.

- I retired.
- I am now an author.

My list is nothing fancy, nothing to put up in lights, but I feel fairly good about it.

What does your list look like?

Here's the thing: Do I really think this list carries any weight outside my own mind? Please.

The truth is, no one really cares about my list of accomplishments. And if I'm honest, do I care about anyone else's? Except said seven children's, of course.

Here's another truth I must face as I wrap that fig leaf around my body and smooth the leaves into place.

When I meet God in the flesh—Jesus—after I leave this world for the next, that list will not go with me. It's hard, I know. I worked on that list from the time I could lisp the words *I did it all by myself*. I've taken it everywhere with me for a long time.

As I'm sure you've done.

First of all, God's already seen my list, and He already knows about the fig leaf. He knows everything, remember? And here's something else even harder to accept.

He doesn't care about my list—He probably cares less about my list than you do.

Ouch!

There is only one thing that will carry any weight with God on that day when I see Him, and it's not on my list. Why?

Because it's not my accomplishment—it's His. I didn't do it. He did.

What am I talking about? You know.

It involves a star, a barnyard, a few straggly shepherds, a

host of angels, a cross, and a tomb. He accomplished what no other human, animal, or being could do.

He washed my heart and changed my mind. He destroyed that meager list of accomplishments, nailing it and all my rebellion to His hands and feet, absorbing the consequences I should have suffered.

He reminded me that the only reason I have anything on my list is because He gave me the ability.

He gives me the *want-to*. He fires my imagination. He allows me to see my little corner of the world with new eyes, a new perspective, and new goals.

He reminds me to look up, not down—at my list.

He says, *Deb—time to trash the Fig Leaf of Hiding Behind Accomplishments. My list is the only one that will count when you get to My country.*

Will you, dear reader, come with me? Will you open your Fig Leaf Closet and pull out your Accomplishments Leaf and hand it over to the One who accomplished eternity for you?

I do hope so.

Questions for Personal Reflection

1. If you made a list of your accomplishments, what would it look like?

   _____

   _____

   _____

   _____

2. Is there anything on your list that God did *not* give you the ability to do?

   _____

   _____

The Fig Leaf Chronicles

---

3. No? Then you know what to do next with your list, right? I'm not saying trash it—I'm saying go down the list and give Him thanks for each one. After all, they're His.

As he journeyed he came near Damascus, and
suddenly a light shone around him from heaven.
Acts 9:3

23

The Fig Leaf of
HIDING BEHIND ADEQUACY

T his isn't something I battle, you say . . . I don't own that
fig leaf. My local Fig Leaf Store doesn't sell that model.
I can do my job, teach my children, be a friend to someone
who needs one, and take care of myself, thank you very much.

I've heard those words before—in my own mind and in my
own voice—as I reassured the folks around me that "I'm just
fine. I don't need your help." But I know better today.

Here's my response to you and to myself: LLPOF!

Remember when we'd say that as children? Back before
text shorthand was a thing?

Liar, liar, pants on fire!

When I was younger, I had the world by the tail. I could get
an A on a test with only one all-nighter the day before . . . and

sometimes with only a half-nighter.

I could eat whatever I wanted and never gain a pound.

I could ace a job interview, body surf in the ocean, sprint down the soccer field, deliver my babies and grow them up, and leap tall buildings in a single bound. Well, maybe not that one.

Like the delusional queen in the fairy tale *Snow White*, I looked at myself in the mirror and saw a five-foot, ten-inch strong, fit woman who sailed through life without a care.

Until I couldn't. Until real life started happening—the one I thought I'd never have to face. And most likely, the one you thought you'd never have to face.

The life that grabs you by the throat and takes things and people away from you in a blink.

The one where one day you wake up and you've been stripped of everything you knew to be true. Now it's twisted into an unrecognizable heap of words you can't lean on, and others in your life ridicule you for still trying to lean on them.

People you thought would never leave you alone and vulnerable—and then they did.

Your own body even betrays you. You can't get to sleep, or you oversleep. You can't enjoy some of your favorite foods . . . or you can and gain ten pounds instead of losing ten pounds.

Your hair thins . . . your joints ache . . . your eyes and ears don't work anymore.

You can't do what you used to do, and you feel your Fig Leaf of Adequacy slip just a bit, threatening to expose to the world what's underneath. Can't have that.

You stand before the mirror and tug and straighten and smooth it down again, trying desperately to convince yourself that *this is not happening to me*. But it is.

Here's the truth, my friends.

Being adequate for life on the earth is an illusion, or a delusion, if you will.

The mirror lies.

I'm barely five foot two, physical strength dwindling each year that passes, and battling unruly hair, skin, and weight. I couldn't whip a five-pound cat, let alone leap a tall building in a single bound.

And I never could. I just thought I could.

Mirror Delusion Syndrome is most often found in young folks, and sometimes it's a good thing. Young people need to believe they can accomplish their mission. They need a gentle push from the older ones in their lives in order to persevere.

If they don't get that, we'll never have another Einstein, Tolkien, Lewis, or Anne Frank.

But at some point in our lives, the blinders come off and we see ourselves the way we really are. If we don't ever come to that point, still believing in our invincibility even into our later years, we end up in a bad place, never placing our trust in anyone else and trying to go it alone but not making it. We all know someone like that—someone who clings to what *was* instead of what *is*. Not a pretty picture.

The apostle Paul spoke to this. Now there was a man who was fit and healthy as a young buck—as he went about jailing believers and delivering them over to the religious authorities for torture and death. Paul was an indispensable tool of the ruling class in the first century AD.

But he had his day, the day he met Jesus and discovered he was wearing the Fig Leaf of Adequacy, trying to hide from God just like our first parents did.

Listen to what he said at the end of Romans 7.

O wretched man that I am! Who will deliver
me from this body of death?
I thank God—through Jesus Christ our Lord!

I'm sure he didn't have a mirror in his hand when he
wrote this, but we get what he was saying. Paul finally saw himself as he truly was, wholly inadequate to do life on his own, in
his own way.

I imagine him thinking back to that day on the Damascus
road.

He stood before Jesus, clad only in his Fig Leaf of Adequacy,
hearing the Lord tell him exactly who he was and exactly who
He was. One of them was God, and it certainly wasn't Paul.

I also imagine that Paul, as he wrote these words years later,
was pleading with us to strip off that Leaf of Adequacy and
allow the Lord Jesus to reclothe us.

Deliver us from this body of death, as it were.

God's wardrobe is always more than adequate—in truth,
perfect—because each item is fashioned by His own hands and
tailor made for each of us. It fits like a glove and is more comfortable than those scratchy leaves, right?

Let's revel in *His* adequacy to lead us through this life and
on into the next. Counting on ourselves is a dead-end proposition.

And downright scary.

Questions for Personal Reflection

1. Look down at yourself right now. Are you wearing your Adequacy Fig Leaf?

   _____

   _____

   _____

   _____

2. Make a list (again) of those tasks you think you're adequate to complete without much strain and stress. Cooking dinner, weeding the garden, shopping? What if you turned that list on its head and admitted you are *not* adequate? That even these mundane tasks need the strength of God for you to complete?

   _____

   _____

   _____

   _____

3. Will you commit to praying—daily—into each task that falls to you, asking God to cover you in His perfect adequacy? I'm right behind you.

   _____

   _____

   _____

   _____

The fear of the LORD is the beginning of knowledge.
Proverbs 1:7

The Fig Leaf of
HIDING BEHIND KNOWLEDGE

Before you get testy, I'll go ahead and say it. Knowledge is not a bad thing. There, we got that out of the way.

But let's pick this apart and talk about what kind of knowledge we hide behind and what kind of knowledge leads to wisdom.

I'll start with Eve.

She had knowledge. But she still found that fig leaf and hid behind it. What do I mean? It depends on the knowledge we're talking about. Knowing who is our current president, or how to fix a car, or where the local park is located isn't bad.

But . . .

Do you remember the tree of the knowledge of good and evil in Eve's story in Genesis? Yeah, that one.

Eve traipsed to her closet—followed by Adam—and both chose the Fig Leaf of Knowledge to wear. Then they did what? They "hid" from God.

Did we hear that right? They thought they could hide from God behind those leaves?

We say to them, how dumb is that? No one, from the oldest person to the one born today, is able to hide from the sovereign Lord of the universe. We can try—and believe me, I have.

Bulletin: it *never* works.

This tree of the knowledge of good and evil opened that inner door of Adam's and Eve's minds to all sorts of things they had no business knowing. Before Eve plucked that fruit and took a bite, then handed one to Adam, they didn't know evil existed, let alone what it was.

That seems weird to us, doesn't it? Evil is all around us. It follows us to the grocery store. It seeps under our front door. And let's not even talk about our television sets—push a button and there's evil in all its gory glory.

But let's talk about how we hide behind knowledge today—how that chic little fig leaf fits us in the modern world.

Here's the deal: knowing who God is and knowing God are two different things.

Millions of people around the globe know who God is. They attend church. They give to charities. They take care of their families and work hard at their jobs. They're good people, no doubt about it. They know who God is and might even voice that knowledge to others.

But . . .

I know who Abraham Lincoln was. I know who our current president is. I know who Stalin was, and Hitler. But I've never met them, and I don't know them. I only know who they are or were.

See the difference?

And what about all those folks we "know" on our social media platforms? Again, knowing about, and knowing, are polar opposites.

Knowledge *about* someone or something is good—but *knowing* is better. *Knowledge about* involves the brain cells; *knowing* involves the heart.

So now we know the difference between *knowing about* and *knowing*. What's next?

The Fig Leaf of Hiding Behind Knowledge is a cunning creation of the Enemy of our souls. Why? Because as long as we're content to just know who God is with no heart involvement, we won't have to get too close to Him or let Him get too close to us. We're under the illusion that we're able to hide from Him. But it's an illusion, as Adam and Eve discovered.

After God kicked them out of their perfect garden, they spent the rest of their lives seeking the closeness they'd once enjoyed with Him and then spurned in one moment of temptation.

Hence, we now have that fig leaf hanging in our closets.

We attend church on Saturday or Sunday and cheat on our time clocks at work.

We say we love others, but the meager time we spend with them tells a different story—and I admit, I am so guilty of this.

We spend money on toys and things we want but neglect those around us who only want their next meal.

Knowing who God is and *knowing God* . . .

Let's strip off that leaf once and for all and let God reveal Himself to us.

Once we do, we'll discover that heart knowledge for which we long, as we dive deep into Him.

Questions for Personal Reflection

1. This is an old question: Do you have head knowledge of God or heart knowledge of Him? Here's a follow-up question: How do you know which one you have?

   _____

   _____

   _____

   _____

2. Where does your heart knowledge of God stop and head knowledge begin?

   _____

   _____

   _____

   _____

3. What one decision will you make today to transform your head knowledge of God into heart knowledge of your Father?

   _____

   _____

   _____

   _____

So when Jesus had received the sour wine,
He said, "It is finished!" And bowing His head,
He gave up His spirit.
John 19:30

25

The Fig Leaf of
HIDING BEHIND GOOD

I see your eyebrows climbing up your forehead. This can't be right. Isn't good . . . good?

Yes, but it's not best.

I'm a list maker, so let's make one.

- Work is good.
- Rest is good.
- Play is good.
- Marriage is good.
- Travel is good.
- Staying home is good.

I see that wrinkled brow. You're wondering where I'm going with this.

Fig leaves are capricious buggers. What do I mean?

I mean that on some days they look stylish—they call to us. I open my closet door and choose the one that glitters the most, the one that looks the most comfortable, and sometimes the one I'm sure won't get me busted.

The Fig Leaf of Hiding Behind Good is the one that won't get me busted. At least, in my own mind. Who can argue with doing good, I ask you?

Well, God for one. He'll take one look at that fig leaf I'm wearing, cover His face with His hands, and moan out my name. *Deb, Deb, Deb, what* are *you wearing? We've talked about this.*

Sounds funny, but it's not really. What does God mean when He says that to me? Or you?

Just this: what we call good is often not His best.

Let's look at that list again.

Work. Working and paying our bills and taking care of our families is good. We're all agreed on that. But what if we flip that on its head, so to speak, and take a harder look.

What if the work we do isn't God's best for us? We make a big deal sometimes out of prospering our families with money and stuff, the safety of a good neighborhood, soccer games and dance classes.

But what if that picture isn't the masterpiece God wants to paint in your life?

What if God has a job for you on the other side of the world? One that is *His best* for you not just your definition of good? A job that will provide an example for your kids of coming out from behind your Fig Leaf of Hiding Behind Good and chasing after His best. One that will leave a legacy of service instead of a legacy of looking good to friends and relatives or of keeping up with the neighbors.

Do you see how pursuing *best* is so much better than settling for *good*?

When Jesus was praying in the garden, He had the same choice to make. How so?

He could've used His God power to destroy His enemies with a word.

Remember this part of the Gethsemane scene?

In John 18:6, He said the words "I Am He," and the soldiers who came to arrest Him face-planted and ate dirt.

Jesus could have done what His followers wanted Him to do—destroy the Roman occupation and set up His kingdom—right then and there.

But He knew something His followers didn't.

It was this: That plan was *good*, might've even been fun, but it was not *best*. What was *best* is illustrated in John 19:30, quoted at the beginning of this chapter.

It was best for Jesus to accomplish His Father's work—which was to go the cross so that His followers could live forever in heaven with Him. As the apostle Paul stated in 1 Corinthians 15:19, "If in this life only we have hope in Christ, we are of all men the most pitiable."

If He'd acquiesced to their *good* plan—a measly political objective—there'd be no eternity in heaven for them or for us.

Are you wearing the Fig Leaf of Hiding Behind Good this moment? If so, run—don't walk—to your closet and exchange it for the clothing He hands you.

Go now. He's waiting for you.

Questions for Personal Reflection

1. What does your "good" list look like?

   _____
   _____
   _____
   _____

2. Contrast that with what your "best" list might look like.

   _____
   _____
   _____
   _____

3. Which one will you throw away?

   _____
   _____
   _____
   _____

But above all these things put on love,
which is the bond of perfection.
Colossians 3:14

The Fig Leaf of

HIDING BEHIND COMPETITION

L ike anything else in this world we call home, competition can be healthy . . . or, not so much. How can we tell the difference?

By the results.

When I was in high school, competition oozed down the walls and soaked into the floorboards in the hallways, the girls' restrooms, and behind the lockers. Some of it was healthy— like on the soccer or football field. Some of it was unhealthy, especially among the girls. High school boys have nothing on high school girls in the arena of unhealthy competition.

I didn't participate in the "my clothes or boyfriend is cuter than yours" skirmishes (mostly because I didn't have any boyfriends or cool, expensive clothes), but I did take my grades seriously. If I received anything less than an A+, my narrow teenage world crumbled around me. I couldn't stand being less than perfect in the grades department.

Again, let's look at our first mom. Eve succumbed to the Competition Leaf from the first moment her finger touched the fruit.

How?

She recognized what that old serpent had clutched in his claw and had to have it. She looked around her beautiful, peaceful home—built especially for her by the owner of the universe—and she wanted more. Eve didn't have neighbors named *the Joneses*, but she might as well have. She ate that shiny morsel in order to keep up with them, so to speak.

That's competition gone awry. And in hers and Adam's case, it was competition on steroids, and unfortunately we inherited the tendency. *Thanks a lot.*

Lest we continue in the mistaken notion that we can blame it all on them, God says we're no better. Adam and Eve had a choice to make. They made the wrong one, no doubt about it.

We have the same choice.

Unhealthy competition and comparisons filter through every crevice in human existence. Look around. Here's a short list:

- politics (a biggie)
- entertainment
- the corporate world
- churches (yes, churches)
- families

If we dissect this list, we see that unhealthy competition leads us down a path we don't want to go—in many instances into broken relationships and even war.

Imagine, if you will, what our world would look like if all of us sought to celebrate one another's successes instead of our own. If our eyes were fixed on Him instead of greedily trying to snatch the fruit out of our colleague's hand.

What a garden of Eden that would be.

The Fig Leaf of Hiding Behind Competition must be exchanged. For what?

For the clothing of mercy, humility, and grace. He stands before us now, offering it to us with His nail-scarred hand.

Reach for *that*, my friend, not for that glittery—but false—Fig Leaf of Competition.

Questions for Personal Reflection

1. What sorts of personal competitions do you indulge in? Are they healthy or unhealthy?

   _____
   _____
   _____
   _____

2. What are the consequences of your unhealthy competitive indulgences, consequences to yourself and to those you love?

   _____
   _____
   _____
   _____

3. How can you replace the unhealthy competitions with healthy ones?

   _____
   _____
   _____
   _____

Godliness with contentment is great gain.
2 Timothy 6:6

The Fig Leaf of
HIDING BEHIND STUFF

As I write this section, the holiday season is just around the corner. Stuff is on my mind, as I'm sure it's on many people's minds.

With the current world situation—no need to go into chaotic detail here—accumulating more stuff is on our minds. But if the world continues to spiral in its present trajectory, the definition of *stuff* will change. Drastically. The stuff we think is critical today likely will not be as important tomorrow.

How much stuff is enough? For much of the world, it's not a lot.

What stuff is essential? Again, in some regions, it might be one pair of worn, too-small shoes. In others, an essential is a fancy-schmancy cell phone.

If you've ever traveled to what society calls a third-world country, you get the idea that piles of stuff aren't really necessary.

I went to Vietnam with a medical team in 2007—it was quite an adventure for a born-and-raised small town girl. I saw sights up close and personal that I'd only ever seen on the news or in a movie.

We set up clinics in small villages in what used to be called North Vietnam. As we traveled in our bus along narrow dirt roads to the next village, we passed groups of people walking to get to the clinic. Barefoot in many cases. These folks had no vehicles or bicycles. But there's something else.

We saw some who couldn't walk for some reason—the elderly, children and babies. They were being carried to the clinic.

I'm not talking about a few blocks. These good people carried their loved ones and neighbors *miles* to see a doctor, to get needed treatment. And some of those who carried others looked as if *they* needed to be carried.

I was never the same after that two-week experience.

When I arrived back at our medium-sized home, which sits on five acres in arid central Washington state, I had a curious reaction. Pulling into the driveway after the long trip home, a flash of guilt coursed through my veins. I had so much.

Doors that closed and locked.

Windows and blinds.

A garage and a vehicle to park in it.

Enough in my personal closet to clothe an entire family.

Food in the kitchen I didn't have to kill first.

Spiders, yes, but normal sized—not ones that looked like

mutants created by a Hollywood special-effects team. I could keep going, but I'm sure you get what I'm saying.

There's something else, though, that I remember about the people I met in Vietnam. Their beaming smiles that could raise the sun right up out of the eastern sky.

Even though—compared to me—they had nothing, they had everything. I had stuff, too much stuff. They had families who loved them enough to physically carry them to receive needed care. Somehow, I wonder if my family members would throw me over their shoulders and trek for miles just to get vitamins or a bandage. In truth, *I* was the one who needed what *they* had, not the reverse.

The Scriptures have much to say about contentment. Like 2 Timothy 6:6 shouting to us that "godliness with contentment is great gain."

Here's the thing: More stuff increases our longing for more stuff. The more we have, the more we want. Then we get more—which leads to wanting more. It's a vicious loop, isn't it?

I think it's time for another trip to my Fig Leaf Closet. Time to yank that one called Hiding Behind Stuff off its hanger and make fertilizer out of it.

Then it'll be time to downsize my stuff pile. After all, what do I really need? Certainly not the six or seven rooms in my house stuffed to the brim with things—including some things that I don't even know why they're there.

Oy!

Can you say fig leaf yard sale?

Questions for Personal Reflection

1. What can you do without? Your first assignment is to make two lists: *Can't Do Without*, and the other *Can Do Without*. Go ahead, we'll wait.

    _____

    _____

    _____

    _____

2. Your second assignment is to review those lists, particularly the *Can't* list. This is just an idea, but is there any chance you can move any items from your *Can't* list to your *Can* list?

    _____

    _____

    _____

    _____

3. And your third assignment is to box up as much from your *Can* list and take the items to a homeless shelter, or your church, or another place where your stuff will do someone else some good. Feeling lighter already, aren't you?

    _____

    _____

    _____

    _____

And He turned and said to them, "If anyone comes to Me and does not hate his father and mother, wife and children, brothers and sisters, yes, and his own life also, he cannot be My disciple."
Luke 14:25, 26

28

The Fig Leaf of
HIDING BEHIND FAMILY

This is a strange one, isn't it?

Let's deal first with the word *hate* in the above verse. Jesus uses it in a comparative sense. We could say it like this:

> If anyone comes to Me and does not hate his
> _____ in comparison to his love for
> Me, He cannot be my disciple.

There's another place in Scripture where Jesus asks an eager disciple to follow him. The disciple wants to wait until he has taken care of his father and mother, then he'll join His traveling ministry.

Jesus says to let the dead bury their dead (Luke 9:60). In

other words, the time to follow Me is now—because there will never come a time on this earth when we are free of human obligations.

Moving into our century, what does our Fig Leaf of Hiding Behind Family look like? It's got several models, and sadly, I own them all.

- I can't talk about Jesus because I might offend one of my family members.
- I can't speak my views, even lovingly, regarding current world events because an argument might ensue.
- I can't voice my opinion about cultural changes around me because I might be labeled a _____.
- I can't do what God has called me to do—whatever that might be—because my family might object . . . for whatever reason.

The first thing I notice about this list is the word *can't*. Why? Because I think, as I look at this list, that it's a cop-out. I'm blaming my family for my *can't dos*. I must turn that on its head and own up to it. They are not to blame. I am.

So to be honest with myself, I must change the word *can't* to *won't*.

Ouch!

The Fig Leaf of Hiding Behind Family doesn't look so shiny to me now. It looks tawdry, dirty with cowardice, and devoid of those holy triplets grace, love, and truth.

We must speak to our family members with respect, and if we disagree, so what? We're allowed to disagree with each other as long as we listen first, then speak the truth with love in our hearts.

As I've said before, we don't always need to speak. In fact, since God gave us one mouth and two ears, we should listen twice as much as we speak.

Our family members might just cut us some slack, right? Can't hurt to find out.

My Fig Leaf Closet is now lighter by several models. Yours?

Questions for Personal Reflection

1. Do you use your fear of confrontation as a shield in order to avoid hard but necessary conversations with your family members?

    _____
    _____
    _____
    _____

2. How do you know if God is asking you to keep silent or to speak up?

    _____
    _____
    _____
    _____

3. How hard would it be for you to choose to serve God with your words to a family member if you thought your loved one might disown you for speaking truth?

    _____
    _____
    _____
    _____

To everything there is a season,
A time for every purpose under heaven.
Ecclesiastes 3:1

29

The Fig Leaf of
HIDING BEHIND TIME

R emember when you were six? Or ten?
Time was an indecipherable concept. Except for the daily givens—time to get up, time to go to school, time for a bath and bed—our child selves were not preoccupied with time's passage.

But fast-forward to today.

Time is a roller coaster careening toward its inevitable end. Or if you're like me, time is a jetliner falling out of the sky. The ground is coming up fast, and I have no control over its speed or crash point.

Humans are funny creatures though. Despite the fact that we know there's a built-in ending, we are still convinced we have time for this or time for that.

Time to hug that person. Time to reconcile with her. Time to lend a hand to someone who needs it. Time to complete that project we started.

Until we don't.

Until we're completely helpless to stop the approaching lights out. We've been able to push Pause a few times, take that medicine, start an exercise program, see that specialist we hope waves a magic wand and makes it go away for a few more months or years.

The truth is, we can push that Pause button only so many times before it breaks and won't work anymore.

Whew! Was that a depressing few paragraphs or what? How can we deal with that—the fig leaf we hide behind called Time?

I think I have the answer.

Do what needs done today. Hug that person. Reconcile with her. Lend that hand. Dive into that project.

Don't let anything stop you from taking care of business today, because the Pause button might break tomorrow.

And for heaven's sake, don't reach for that fig leaf again. March right up to it, yank it out of your closet, and throw it where the sun doesn't shine.

Because if you don't, the next fig leaf you reach for will be . . . well, be sure to read the last chapter of this book . . . You'll get my drift.

Questions for Personal Reflection

1. Be honest—do you ever think seriously about the roller coaster of time you are riding? Do you wake up each morning thinking you have all day to get *that* done?

    _____

    _____

    _____

    _____

2. If you had to make a list of tasks to get done today, would your list look different if you knew—really *knew*—there'd be no tomorrow?

    _____

    _____

    _____

    _____

3. Bouncing off the above question, which line item would you move to the top of your list if you knew you'd have no tomorrow?

    _____

    _____

    _____

    _____

"Have mercy upon me, O God . . . Blot out my transgressions . . . wash me . . . cleanse me . . . against You, You only, have I sinned."
Psalm 51:1–2, 4

The Fig Leaf of
HIDING BEHIND REGRET

U gh. Regret is a uniquely human reaction to events. Animals don't experience it. Why? Because God built regret into the human soul.

Regret is a feeling of sorrow or remorse for a fault, act, loss, disappointment, etc. To that, I'd add *remorse for failing to act*. As the above verse illustrates, even King David, "the man after God's own heart" (1 Samuel 13:14; Acts 13:22), was well acquainted with the sting of regret.

And that brings us to that pesky Fig Leaf of Regret.

You might be wondering what happens when we don this one. In other words, how do we hide behind regret? Let's talk about that.

The Fig Leaf of Regret is a shadowy leaf, barely there, perhaps not even visible to others around us. Maybe all they can see is the barest outline of the leaf encircling us.

But, boy howdy, they sure pick up on it. You might be wondering how they know it's there if it's so barely there.

It's because of how we behave when we're wearing it. What do I mean? I'll give you a personal example, because I have many regrets. Yep, I surely do. Then, let's talk about how to do life without that cloud hanging over us.

In chapter 1 I told you about losing my sister to suicide in 1989. What I didn't tell you was what had happened years before.

When I was a young adult living in California, with toddlers of my own, Holly was about seventeen. I found out from my parents during a phone call that she'd been involved in some things that weren't good. My reaction at the time was appropriate—I was sad over it. But what I did next makes me cringe to this day.

In the days following that phone call, I became more and more angry at what she'd done. One day I called her. It didn't go well. Her response to my big-sisterish "meddling"—as she called it—was not what I wanted.

I wanted her to at least acknowledge her wrongdoing, but heavy handed as I was, she backed away from that step. Big surprise there, you might be thinking. But at the time, I was too righteously indignant and too much of a control freak to see it.

So what did I do? I refused to talk to her. For how long? Years.

We did eventually reconcile, but for me, the damage was done and came into full bloom during the weeks and months after her death. To this day I still get a whiff of those blooms of regret in my own life. I can't even contemplate what my harshness did to her.

Bottom line? The Fig Leaf of Regret is a noxious weed, spreading and taking over fertile ground in your soul until there's no room for anything else. If we let it take root, it will spread seeds of pain with every footfall.

So is regret all bad? No. It's a warning sign.

It says *Danger—turn around and go back*. Back where? Back to the arms of the loving God who stripped off the fig leaves of our first parents and clothed them in his own skin of mercy and grace. But first make a stop at your closet, take that Fig Leaf of Regret, and put it in His hands to deal with.

You won't regret that.

Questions for Personal Reflection

1. Everyone has regrets, so I won't ask you if have any. But I will ask you to think through one regret you have and then examine how it affects you and possibly your loved ones today.

    _____
    _____
    _____
    _____

2. Think about that age-old concept *if only I could go back in time, I'd* _____. Well, you can't, can you? So what can you do about that monstrous regret you feel?

    _____
    _____
    _____
    _____

3. Were you able to answer the above question? Perhaps not. If we don't know what to do with the agony of long-ago regrets, let's step away from our Fig Leaf Closets and lay those regrets at the feet of the only One in the universe who has the answers we need to hear.

    _____

    _____

    _____

    _____

A NOTE FROM DEB

This was a fun and often lighthearted treatment of the darkest day in human history. The day that ushered blackness into God's newly created world—a world lit by His presence.

Imagining Adam and Eve fussing over how to put those dang fig leaves on—adjusting, trying to keep them from falling off and revealing something ugly underneath, draping them over their . . . ahem . . . private parts—was what started this project rolling in my head.

Can you see them? They'd just thumbed their noses at the creator and sustainer of the universe, and now they're hiding from Him and worrying about how to make fig leaves become a wardrobe. Really?

We see them and we think, *What in the world are you doing? This won't work. Hello, He already knows!*

But isn't that who we are?

We say that word, or we don't. We look at that image. We refuse to do what we're told, like we're two years old again. And just like them, we play the blame game.

We must face the fact that we are them.

But there's another fact we have to face.

We're still playing the blame game. You know what I mean. We blame them for our fig leaves, don't we? It's their fault that rebellion against God is in my DNA—isn't that what we say sometimes to justify ourselves?

Another lie, my friends.

Let's just stop, okay? How about we empty our Fig Leaf Closets and never wear them again. I like that plan. You?

Encountering Jesus amid our flawed lives, we discover He is bigger than our rebellion, our tragedies, and our confusion.

This devotional plunges you into the lives of twelve biblical characters who are mentioned briefly, almost parenthetically, as the stories of well-known players are told. Several of these obscure individuals aren't even named. But God included them in His Word for a reason, and the reason is us. Author Deb Gorman puts flesh on the bones of these shadow people, to name them, to fill in the canvas of their lives so spiritual truths can be extracted.

So, get ready to meet these personalities in a new way. And the next time you're tempted to think your life is insignificant, that God can't use such a flawed, mistake-ridden person such as yourself, remember: these twelve people probably thought the same, and here you are reading their stories and learning powerful lessons from their encounters with God. God created you to impact others, and that is definitely not insignificant!

The path of your life will change each time you hold fast to your faith.

This book is about choices. If there is one thing universal in the human experience, it's that we make choices every day. Our choices range from determining how much we'll spend for a cup of coffee to whom we'll spend the rest of our lives with, but only one choice determines where we'll spend eternity.

This devotional immerses you into the lives of six biblical characters whom God brought to the sharp point of radical decisions—decisions that would change the course of their earthly existences. We might think these six people have nothing to do with us in our century of instant communication, driverless cars, and computers mounted on our wrists, but the earth is old, and humankind hasn't changed.

The choices we make each day still determine the next moment, the next year, the next millennium and have far-reaching consequences for the next generation. God included these characters in His Word for a reason, and the reason is us.

Have you ever confronted a fork in the road of life and paused, wondering which way to go? Or maybe you took the path that seemed most logical, without much thought.

Perhaps the new direction was the correct one . . . but perhaps not. What do you do if you travel the wrong path?

Read the stories of thirteen people from the Bible who stood at the fork and made a choice. See where their journeys took them.

Pause that the fork in your own road and make the right decision, not just for the here and now but for future generations—your children, grandchildren, and generations beyond, doomed to suffer the consequences of a wrong choice and who scream silently at you to go back.

And if you discover you're on the wrong road, don't believe the lie that you can't turn back.

For the first terror-filled step into the great divide will lay out a cross-shaped bridge before you, stained with holy blood—the sure road that will lead you back to the beginning, where you will find grace to start again.

A novel of human brokenness and God's still-unfolding drama of redemption . . .

When two wounded and dysfunctional families wind up unexpectedly at the remote Master's Inn during a December snowstorm, it's up to owners Tom and Barb Masters to help—except they're dealing with their own bitter issues. As the winter snowfall confines them, the three families find themselves coping with their crippled relationships and hard emotions . . . and sometimes tearing one another down in the process.

But when a tragic secret is inadvertently revealed and a rebellious teenage girl takes off into the storm, chaos descends. Will they be tossed into more heartbreak, or will the crisis draw them together against a common enemy?

With a forest in Washington state as the backdrop, join Tom and Barb at their B&B as they strive to show Christ's love to all who cross their threshold . . . even when it threatens their own sanity and safety.

Deb contributed to this *Chicken Soup for the Soul* anthology, which includes 101 inspirational, compassionate, and empowering stories to help you cope with loss, regain your strength, and find joy in life again.

Losing a loved one is hard. It doesn't matter who it is, it creates a hole in your life.

I lost my only sister to suicide in 1989, and that hole in my heart and in my family is still there.

With these 101 stories, including a short story about my sister, you'll find people just like you who have loved and lost, and have learned how to live, love, and even laugh again.

One today is worth two tomorrows. ~Ben Franklin

By the time Thursday is over, Annie Lee is convinced God is telling her it's her last day on earth.

Annie and her husband, along with their four children, live in a small rural town in central Washington state—a place where almost nothing scary ever happens . . . until today.

Hang on to her coattails as she navigates her tragic past, her frightening present, and her unknown future in the space of twenty-four hours.

Ask yourself the same question posed to Annie: "What would I do today if I knew I'd die tomorrow?"

Will your answer be the same one Annie discovers?

ABOUT THE AUTHOR

Deb Gorman, author and owner of Debo Publishing, was born and reared in the beautiful Pacific Northwest. She still lives in her hometown with her husband, Alan, and their very smart German Shepherd, Hoka.

Deb is a follower of the Lord Jesus Christ, cleverly disguised as a wife, mom, grandmom, and author. Her purpose is to connect with God's most beautiful and clever creation, the human family, using the literary talent and imagination God gave her.

Her prayer is that as she journeys together with you, we will discover encouragement and redemption in our most important relationships. Connect with Deb at https://debggorman.com where you will find her blog posts and information about her books, both published and upcoming.